GREEN-BELT CITIES

GLEN OAKS COLLEGE LIBRARY

GREEN-BELT CITIES

by
Frederic J. Osborn

new edition
Foreword by Lewis Mumford

SCHOCKEN BOOKS · NEW YORK

First SCHOCKEN *edition 1969*
Second Printing, 1971

© *Frederic J. Osborn,* 1946 *and* 1969
Library of Congress Catalog Card No. 77-85678

Manufactured in the United States of America

CONTENTS

DIAGRAMS IN THE TEXT   *page* vii
ACKNOWLEDGMENTS   viii
FOREWORD BY LEWIS MUMFORD   ix
PREFATORY AFTERTHOUGHTS   I
AUTHOR'S INTRODUCTION   13

PART ONE

THE GARDEN CITY MOVEMENT
A REVALUATION

I. EBENEZER HOWARD AND THE GARDEN CITY IDEA
    The Problem of Urban Aggregation   25
    A New Conception of the Town   27
    The 'Unique Combination of Proposals'   32
II. THE BATTLE OF MODERN PLANNING THOUGHT
    The Idea Submerged   36
    The Period of Confusion   40
    The New 'Symbiosis'   46

PART TWO

THE WORKING MODELS EXAMINED

III. THE PHYSICAL PATTERN
    Choice and Purchase of Sites   56
    The Garden City Companies   58
    First Stages: Survey and Plan   60
    Engineering Considerations   62
    Landscape Gardening and Tree Planting   65
    Agricultural Considerations   68
    Evolution of the Town Plan   69
IV. THE LAND: ITS USE AND CONTROL
    Planning through Lease Covenants   72
    Industrial Development   76
    Retail Trade and Shopping Policy   83
    Public Buildings, Schools and Open Spaces   89
    Residential Areas: Layout and Densities   91

CONTENTS

V. ADMINISTRATION, LOCAL GOVERNMENT AND FINANCE
Administration:
Control of Use and Appearance   96
Local Government   104
Garden City Finance: Housing Subsidies   106
IV. SOCIAL LIFE AND CULTURE   113

PART THREE
GREEN-BELT CITIES: THE FUTURE
VII. A NATIONAL POLICY OF DISPERSAL
The Meaning of Dispersal   131
Scale and Pace of Dispersal   133
VIII. WAYS AND MEANS OF DISPERSAL
The Siting of New Towns   141
Promotion and Finance of New Towns   148
Getting the New Communities Going   154
Expansion of Existing Country Towns   158
Local Government and its Boundaries   160
The Technique of Town Development   165
APPENDICES   167
NOTES TO NEW EDITION   185
SELECT BIBLIOGRAPHY   195
INDEX   199

DIAGRAMS IN THE TEXT

A typical Levitical city   *page* 168
Layout of Jerusalem and its permanent
  reservations   170
Sir Thomas More's Utopia   173
New Towns in Great Britain   179

ACKNOWLEDGMENTS

In the first edition of this book I thanked for information and help the persons mentioned on page 55, and in addition Councillor L. W. Bennett, M.B.E., Robert Bennett, F.R.I.B.A., C. M. Crickner, F.R.I.B.A., Bernard Ellis, W. H. Gaunt, C.B.E., Dr. Norman Macfadyen, M.B., Barry Parker, F.R.I.B.A., C. S. Pratt, F.S.I., J. D. Ritchie, J. D. Rowland and R. W. Tabor (all of Letchworth); and Charles Dalton, H. France, Mrs. Lilian Houghton, Paul Mauger, F.R.I.B.A., and Fred Page (of Welwyn Garden City).

For encouragement and co-operation in this revision I am indebted to Lewis Mumford, who contributes a foreword, and to Michael Hughes, of Welwyn Garden City, who has generously assisted me in many ways.

1969   FJO

FOREWORD

After Ebenezer Howard's *Garden Cities of Tomorrow*, *Green-Belt Cities* stands as the classic statement of the garden city idea, now better known, if less faithfully interpreted, as the new towns movement. Those who are becoming acquainted with this movement for the first time – and an awakening to the need for this approach to urban planning has now become worldwide – will find no better introduction to its basic principles and purposes than Sir Frederic Osborn's *Green-Belt Cities*.

Green-Belt Cities was written in 1945, at a critical point in the formulation of public planning and housing policy. The evidence gathered by the pre-war Barlow Committee, re-enforced by the massive urban bomb damage suffered during the war, resulted in the acceptance by all parties of a policy of national planning, and this in turn led under a Labour Government to the report of the New Towns (Reith) Committee and the passage of the New Towns Act in 1946. Many able minds contributed to this outcome; but if any one person deserves credit for bringing about this great change, that credit belongs to Osborn.

As early as 1918, in *New Towns After the War*, Osborn had pointed out the folly of random housing and aimless town extension in ever more congested and disorganized urban conglomerations. As spokesman for an *ad hoc* 'National Garden Cities Committee', which comprised Ebenezer Howard, C. B. Purdom, W. G. Taylor and himself, he pleaded for the building of a hundred new towns. The response to this plea was delayed a quarter-century, and the number of towns promoted by the New Towns Act still falls badly short of the 1918 goal and still more of present needs. But some thirty new towns have been designated, and the first fifteen are now firmly established. As a result of their success the basic idea of new towns, in one form or another, is spreading rapidly throughout the world.

This fresh wave of new towns bears witness to Sir Frederic Osborn's far-sightedness, his tireless persistence in presenting the

FOREWORD

case for green-belt cities – an alternate designation for garden cities – and not least to the inherent soundness of the new towns policy itself. Though Osborn, with Arnold Whittick, has published an important coda to this book, in a detailed description and analysis of the new towns that have actually been built, *Green-Belt Cities* is still the best summary of the essential ideas behind the new towns movement. More than that: this book embodies valuable experience in coping with planning, administrative, technical and social problems, which he himself had acquired as estate manager and resident in Welwyn Garden City.

The core idea of the garden city, as a varied, many-sided, balanced, integrated urban environment, with biological, economic and social advantages that urban overgrowth had destroyed, was tested out, under far from favourable conditions, by the first two garden cities, which were private enterprises, unsupported by government funds. Without that experimental demonstration the further development of new towns would have been difficult, if not impossible. The original conception of green-belt cities will be modified by further experience and elaborated under the pressure of new needs and the stimulus of new opportunities. But behind these changes will remain both Howard's and Osborn's vision: the marriage of town and country, in an increasingly coherent urban and regional pattern.

LEWIS MUMFORD

America, New York
(*1st October, 1968*)

PREFATORY AFTERTHOUGHTS

Readers should be aware that the main part of this book (pages 13 to 184) was written nearly a quarter-century ago, just before the appointment of the official committee that led to the New Towns Act of 1946. The text has been reproduced photographically without any alteration. It must be taken therefore as a statement of the views, proposals and hopes of an advocate of the new towns policy before any governmental action on it had begun.

Since then there have been great changes in our society – economic, political and cultural – and notably in town planning powers, theory and practice. I think my diagnosis and prescription for the major maladies of cities remains in essence sound. But if I were writing the book today many passages in it would be re-worded, a few in fact retracted.

To bring the record of events (and my own argument) more up-to-date I have added these Afterthoughts, and a series of Notes (pages 185–194) numbered according to the paragraphs in the original text to which they refer. The footnotes in that text are unchanged.

The book-list has been enlarged to include some useful recent publications, but the literature of new towns has now become so considerable that the list remains highly selective.

New Towns under the 1946 Act

The implementation of a national policy of "decongestion and dispersal", as recommended by the report (1940) of the (Barlow) Royal Commission on the Distribution of the Industrial Population, began with the appointment of the official New Towns Committee, which produced in 1945–46 three lucid and positive reports. Immediately thereafter Lewis (now Lord) Silkin, then Minister of Town and Country Planning, introduced the first New Towns Act, which was passed with all-party support. The

PREFATORY AFTERTHOUGHTS

Reith Committee had suggested several possible types of agency for the construction of new towns, with preference for an *ad hoc* "development corporation" for each town; and it was this method alone that was adopted in the 1946 Act.[1] Each corporation was to consist of up to nine persons appointed by the Minister, empowered to purchase a sufficient area of land, compulsorily if necessary, and to develop it on an approved plan. It would have all the common-law powers and rights of an ordinary land-owner, and in addition a few others needed for the special case of complete town development, such as statutory planning powers and entitlement to public housing subsidies. Each was to be financed by 60-year government loans at current rates of interest and repayment. The initial authorization was for advances to a maximum of £50 million. (Under later Acts up to 1968 this has been increased to £1,100 million.)

The first six new towns were designated within a year and a further eight by 1950. In the following 10 years, owing to a regrettable change in government policy, only one was started (Cumbernauld, 1955). In 1961, however, designations were resumed, and by the end of 1968 28 towns were in progress in Great Britain and two, under similar legislation, in Northern Ireland.

While the first new towns were planned for ultimate populations of 25,000 to 50,000 each, the targets of the first 15 have since been enlarged – to an average of about 75,000. Their original populations averaged about 7,500, so they are now intended to accommodate an "intake" of about a million people, and up to the end of 1968 they absorbed about 600,000, mostly drawn from overcrowded cities. These 15 are now firmly established as well-equipped industrial and commercial towns in which the majority of inhabitants find employment at short distances from good modern houses with gardens.

The creation in an old country of 15 new towns planned for a million people is on the face of it impressive. But it is a very modest achievement in relation to the scale of needed decongestion and the rate of growth of the total population. The programme has therefore been stepped up, and many of the latest new towns

[1]The text of the 1946 Act is printed in C. B. Purdom's *Building of Satellite Town*, 1949.

commissioned are being planned for up to 100,000 each, and in some cases as "cluster-cities" up to 250,000 or more. Altogether the first 30 new towns may be capable of providing for about $2\frac{1}{2}$ million people by the end of the century.

When, in the first edition of *New Towns After the War* (1918), I demanded a national programme of 100 towns of 40–50,000 I felt more logical than realistic; and in the reissue of 1942 I timidly reduced the specification to 50 towns, for say 2 million people. At that time however there was national alarm about the decline in the birth-rate, and a Royal Commission in 1949 warned Britain that, unless something drastic was done, our population would reach a peak in 1980, and thereafter begin to fall catastrophically. In the first edition of this book (pages 134–5) I used as one of the arguments for new towns that their form of housing might save the race from the threat of extinction; and Lewis Mumford, in several of his writings, did the same. Whether or not the reproduction rate is really affected by high or low density, that particular argument carries no weight now; and I am not so rash as to reverse it by pointing to the surprising fact that in Welwyn Garden City – where family houses with gardens prevail – the latest birth-rate figure is *below* the national average.

All the expert estimates, for the world as well as for Britain, now predict, on present trends, a huge "population explosion". Those for the end of this century (a doubled world population and a growth of 15 to 20 millions for Great Britain) may I think reasonably be doubted in view of the reversed alarm, but a large increase in the next 15 to 20 years is virtually certain, unless the human race essays to destroy itself by atomic warfare, or micro-organisms are clever enough to defeat us in the inter-species struggle.

For the United Kingdom, even if we accept the lower estimates of population growth, the present new towns programme is clearly inadequate. The first 15 towns are slowing down in intake as they approach completion and are unlikely to provide for more than 30,000 persons a year; while the latest 15, at 4,000 a year each (which is rather rapid for social assimilation), might take another 60,000 a year. The national population growth is many times greater, and with the advance of affluence the space demands of the families still penned up in old cities must expand.

3

Where are all these millions to go? Some can with advantage be accepted by existing towns of moderate size; but there is a limit to their capacity if good standards are to be observed. Obviously Britain must start many more new towns. But I attempt no fresh numerical specification.

Success of Corporation System

One of the chief lessons of the British experiment is the efficiency of the development corporation, governmentally appointed and financed, yet endowed with a high degree of autonomy. Essentially this has the merits of Ebenezer Howard's limited-dividend company owning the freehold of an entire town estate and disposing of sites for defined uses to public and private enterprises within it – an invention no less important than his physical formula for the "marriage of town and country". It not only makes possible the thoughtful planning of each town in answer to local economic, topographical and social considerations, and of variety in form and character, but it also enables the increment of land value resulting from population growth to be conserved for the improvement of the estate or other public purposes. It is a machinery appropriate to the "mixed economy" towards which both free-enterprise and collectivist states seem to be feeling their way, with or without approval by doctrinaires in either camp.

Founding a new town, like planting a forest, is a long-term enterprise unattractive to investors who look for a return within a few years. But inside a town there are opportunities for investment in buildings and equipment which can be remunerative almost from the start, as many manufacturing and commercial businesses great and small, and many owner-occupiers of houses, have found. Most of the largest industrial corporations, national and international, and the major retail organisations, as well as many new ones, have established factories, shops and offices (in some cases their headquarters) in the new towns. Indeed, after a hesitant period, the rate of settlement and expansion of businesses has in a number of cases outpaced that of housing for workers, and the admittance of further firms has had to be restrained.

Already the intriguing problem of the means of limiting a new town's ultimate population is in sight.

New Towns as a Public Investment

In the first edition I claimed that new towns could pay their way (see pp. 152–158), but I was not able to say that the two pioneer garden cities had yet done so. That rubicon has since been crossed. Both have passed into public ownership after their companies had, for different reasons, abandoned Howard's principle of a limit on profits; and both, on the public take-overs, yielded their companies a substantial capital surplus. That this benefited the investors instead of the towns' inhabitants as originally intended is regrettable, but the more important fact is that the profitability of the system of unified ownership of a town estate was proved.

This has been confirmed by the financial record of the first twelve government-sponsored towns in England and Wales. By 1959, at an average age of 11 years, collectively they broke even, after covering interest and repayments from the start, and by 1967 they were yielding a surplus of the order of £2 million a year – all initial costs having been paid off.[1] Besides this, they have saved the nation millions in housing construction costs and subsidies as compared with the alternative of multi-storey flats in big cities.

The Technique of Town Building

When the first corporations were appointed there were no experts in building complete towns *de novo* except a few survivors of the original Letchworth and Welwyn teams. Finding suitable members and staff must have severely taxed the judgment of ministers and their advisers. They caught a few duds, but on the whole I think they chose pretty well. I admit I was at first shocked by the

---

[1]Full accounts are published in the official annual reports of the corporations, and are summarized in the January numbers of *Town and Country Planning* (1956 to date).

magnitude of their staff and overhead expenses compared with the economical establishments of the two pioneer garden cities. To some extent this was justified by the faster speed of development expected and achieved. But they made some costly mistakes that I am sure would have been avoided if the corporations had had access to a central advisory body as recommended by the Reith Committee. The reports of that committee were, I have often been told, extremely helpful to the corporations, but the "know-how" of a complex business cannot be fully conveyed even in the most competent text book. Lord Silkin, the "true begetter" of the New Towns Act, rejected this Reith recommendation in fear that it might lead to undue standardization of plans. In the event, however, a less informed standardization was imposed by civil service personnel who themselves necessarily lacked town-building "know-how", yet had powers of veto that a purely advisory body would not have possessed.

Theoretically autonomous as the corporations were, many have complained that they were kept too tightly in leading strings, especially by financial controls on details of expenditure. It could be said on the other hand that the central control squashed some silly or extravagant proposals. A number of these however did slip through. When the fancy for an untried idea or a fashionable gimmick infects both an adventurous corporation personnel and a suzerain ministry remote from the consumer, serious mistakes result, and it is the people catered for who suffer. This did occasionally happen. Still, everybody learns by doing, and there are now, as there were not when I wrote this book or the Reith Committee sat, hundreds of practised town-builders who can tell me more than I can tell them. If they read this reissue, it will probably be more for anecdotal interest or amusement than for enlightenment. I am trying to pass on, as well as my own experience, what I have learned from theirs.

Success of the First New Towns

By the end of 1968, more than 900,000 people were living in the first 22 new towns in Great Britain. Fifteen of these had then reached a stage at which their character as urban communities

6

could be discerned. They differ greatly in detail, not only physically but economically, socially and culturally. But they are all primarily manufacturing centres, in which, as in the country as a whole, roughly half the population work in industry and the other half in trading, services and professions. There is, of course, some interchange of employment with nearby towns and rural districts, the workers who come in from outside being more numerous than those who go out. The impression given by some writers that they are dormitory suburbs is untrue. Such commuting as exists is mostly of short range, to and from places within 5 to 7 miles,[1] and some of this is due to obstacles to changes of residence in a condition of housing shortage.

The new towns have provided modern dwellings of the popularly desired type in healthy, spacious and pleasantly landscaped surroundings, first-class public services, schools, and a modicum of essential community facilities. As they have grown, excellent shopping centres and a widening range of additional amenities, social, educational and cultural, have developed. The initial scantiness of the institutions and services characteristic of long established towns has been criticized, and no doubt the more generous and earlier provision of some of these, for example of buildings for assembly and group activities, would have been justified in advance of full demand. But criticism in this field has been at once purblind and over-acute. It overlooks the fact that this was a substantial human migration, that like all migrations it depended first and foremost on finding the means to live and secondarily, as Plato said, the means to live more abundantly. Throughout history, human settlements have normally begun with primitive shelter, and only over a period have they risen to a high degree of civilization and culture. These new towns, unlike settlements of the past, had from their very beginning good dwellings, roads, water, sewerage, gas, electricity and postal services, newspapers, telephones, radio, schools, churches, and at least some meeting places in which they could exchange their own skills in music, outdoor and indoor games, dancing and any kind of do-it-yourself activity. They had first-class places of employ-

---

[1]*Sample Census 1966, Workplace and Transport Tables Part 1.* H.M.S.O. 1968
F. J. Osborn: "New Towns Self-Containment", *Town and Country Planning,*
Oct. - Nov., 1968.

ment close by at good rates of pay. What by comparison had the migrants to new towns of the Middle Ages or the Industrial Revolution? Or the millions of commuters to new suburban housing estates?

Innumerable surveys and studies of the people in the new towns have been made. They are continuously under the sociologist's microscope and the psychologist's X-ray probe. Obviously these find a percentage of discontented and ill-adjusted persons, as they would find anywhere. And obviously there are some inhabitants who on particular details like their new situations less than their former ones. Most of these say: "Yes, the surroundings are fine and my job good enough, but . . ." and they describe something they miss, which they sense their questioners are specially keen to elicit. In any migration, from anywhere to anywhere, individuals will similarly testify. Changes of environment and breaks in personal association are welcome to some and distressing to others. But given that migration is inevitable, as for many reasons it is, what alternative location more acceptable to the majority of people is conceivable than these new towns? How can any social scientist weigh the subjective experiences of an unascertained percentage of people who really enjoy these surroundings and through familiarity have come to take them for granted, with those of a percentage who are more conscious of varying deprivations? And how far can we evaluate the degrees in which the satisfactions will be long-term and the dissatisfactions temporary?

To me it is a matter of plain commonsense that for the great majority of people the new towns offer a far more pleasing environment than crowded and squalid quarters in old cities, from which in any case large numbers must be dispersed. The only alternative is a further sprawl of suburbs which could give a pleasant environment for dwellings, but at the expense of longer and longer daily journeys to work, and the further banishment of the open country from those locked up in great cities. And, I think, a smaller chance of a healthy advance in urban culture.

Of course the new towns are not perfect, either as structures or communities. We advocates are sometimes taunted as blue-eyed idealists who set out to produce "Heavens below" and have failed. But we didn't, and we haven't. We made out a case for a more sensible, healthy, and comfortable distribution of population than either urban coagulation or sprawl; explained why it was necessary; by experiment showed that it was practicable; and proposed political machinery by which it could be done.

It has been done: the machinery works; and it has been proved that new towns can be economically viable, industrially and commercially efficient, and even in their early stages pleasant and acceptable to most of their inhabitants. Socially and culturally they improve as they grow, and as examples they pave the way to still better towns. Not that every new town is necessarily an advance on its predecessors. Some have in fact, under the influence of the 'land-saving' obsession of the 1950's (see Note 45) and socially insensitive architectural fashions, needlessly lowered their space standards, and some, in pursuit of experimental novelty, have made serious mistakes. These are likely to be corrected as popular opinion asserts itself.

The pioneer new towns certainly suffer from a shortage of private garages and public parking space; the magnitude of the expansion of car-use was not foreseen. Their open layout does however make the problem less insoluble than in densely packed cities, though the lines of moving and waiting cars in centres and residential areas seriously detract from safety and visual amenity. In later plans it is assumed that people of all income groups will own private cars, and provision is made or space reserved for at least one car per dwelling; and both in town centres and residential areas efforts are made to separate as far as practicable vehicular and pedestrian traffic. Much study and experiment has been devoted to housing layouts, which (contrary to some critical impressions) exhibit much greater variety than in any other post-war development. There is still a tendency to tailor town plans too tightly to known present requirements or to apply standards that people from crowded cities will just tolerate – for example in garden space. The private garden is valued, not only for hobby cultivation, but for a pleasing outlook, a wide angle of light from sun and sky, privacy from peering passers-by, safety for children under the eye of the mother, drying clothes, and as an outdoor room. If cut too small it ceases to have the desired "garden" feeling. As affluence grows some people can afford and will prefer to have some of their surrounding open space cultivated for them, but the total amount should not be reduced. Now that garages are almost universal the old official maximum of 12 houses an acre is far from extravagant, and other needs may arise. Planners should always leave some margin of space for the unforeseen.

It is not possible in this book to discuss at length the vast issues of regional development now emerging in Britain and other countries, and of the economic planning that for many reasons has to be integrated with the physical planning in which new towns must obviously play an important part. These have now become topics of world-wide political interest and controversy, and many states which confront or have in prospect problems of urban aggregation and congestion are impressed by the British new towns initiative and are studying it intently. If we have, historically, the credit of pioneering the Industrial Revolution, with its immense potential for raising the living standards of the human race, we also have the discredit of some of its lamentable consequences in the character of industrial towns. It is therefore appropriate that we have given something of a lead towards better forms of urban development. But we ourselves have a long way to go.

F.J.O.

Welwyn Garden City, 1969

GREEN-BELT CITIES

INTRODUCTION

This book is concerned with a strangely neglected social issue: that of the size of towns and the disposition of towns in relation to the countryside. There is, in my view, no social issue more important. Space for living is one of the primary human needs, and the ration of space obtainable by dwellers in towns is dependent on the physical arrangement of their houses, workplaces and other buildings. It is a matter of common observation that large cities are always crowded cities; it is not so well realized that, in the absence of some measure of planned control, they must be so. The degradation of living-space standards, and especially of the standard of space available for the family home and its garden, is only one of the penalties of neglect of the subject. Among many others are the increasing burden of suburban journeys, the cutting-off of millions of townspeople from access to the countryside, and the disintegration of local community life.[*]

'The sights and sounds of everyday life affect everyone,' said Victor Hugo: and indeed it is hardly possible to over-estimate the influence of habitual surroundings on the quality of human personality and the character of society. On the young the influence is decisive and lifelong. Walt Whitman, a poet of interest in the present context because he is poised between enthusiasm for the multitudinous city and passionate love of the countryside, constantly recurs to this theme:

There was a child went forth every day,
And the first object he look'd upon, that object he became,
And that object became part of him for the day or a certain part
    of the day,
Or for many years or stretching cycles of years.
The early lilacs became part of this child,
And grass, and red and white morning-glories, and white and red
    clover. . . .
And all the changes of city and country wherever he went . . .

13

They became part of that child who went forth every day,
And who now goes, and will always go forth every day.[1]

And a writer of our time expresses the same truth with almost
sociological precision:

'Men and women are not only themselves; they are also the
region in which they were born, the city apartment or the farm
in which they learnt to walk, the games they played as children,
the old wives' tales they overheard, the food they ate, the schools
they attended, the sports they followed, the poets they read, and
the God they believed in.'[2]

This is a terrifying realization for anyone who is familiar with
the vast areas of squalor in our cities, which still bear witness
that in the early phases of industrialism the environmental interests of the masses of people were entirely disregarded. The obsession
was with creating the great productive machine with which we
are now blessed. 'Men were so engrossed in building mills that
towns were left to build themselves.'[3] With the rise of democracy,
education, trade unionism and social compunction many of the
evils of industrialism—child labour, long hours, sweated wages,
insanitary housing, dangerous factory processes, and so on—have
been abolished or mitigated, largely by legislative regulation. The
principle of governmental intervention has indeed proved so indispensable in dealing with them that it has become almost a
popular religion, and none the less a valid one because we are now
conscious that the principle has limits.

It is more than odd that the last of the evils of industrialism to
come under discussion as a possible subject of social control, or
even of collective forethought, is one of the greatest—the size and
related density of towns. Trust in the 'invisible hand' of economic
theory to look after the distribution of population and industry
was all of a piece with the 'individualist' philosophy that fought
a hundred-years' rearguard action against the more 'socialist'
ideology of the working-men's movements. These movements
made the pace in social advance in many other fields; and I rank
it as a disaster of the first magnitude that they shared the general

[1] *Autumn Rivulets: There was a child went forth.*
[2] W. Somerset Maugham: *The Razor's Edge* (1944).
[3] J. L. and Barbara Hammond, *The Town Labourer* 1760–1832 (1917).

blindness to the trends of town development. The trust, amounting almost to complacency, that the size of towns and the location of industry could be left to take care of themselves, became universal and still largely persists. It extended to the statesmen and leaders of all parties, including labour and socialist thinkers who, on all other issues, certainly did not discount the potentialities of social control and collective forethought.*

Much avoidable damage has been done by this consensus of fatalism. We are well into an era of building and rebuilding. In this century, and especially since the first World War, most industrial countries have engaged in an immense amount of housing, and, for the first time in history, the accent has been on the provision of good dwellings for the industrial masses. In Great Britain, something like one-third of the population live in the four and a half million houses built since 1920. But, owing to the entire absence of awareness of the issue of the size and distribution of towns, or of belief that these matters can come under human control, we have allowed state finance and public housing energy to continue and accelerate one of the most destructive tendencies of the industrial revolution—the massing of our population in excessively large and perniciously congested cities.

In 1939 we had reached the point in Great Britain that two-fifths of our entire population were living and working in seven great agglomerations; more than one-fifth indeed in the single agglomeration of London. Great Britain is only the extreme case of a world-wide phenomenon, due everywhere to the same supine neglect of the subject by thinkers and leaders of all social and political schools. Their fatalism was no doubt encouraged by the fact that the phenomenon is world-wide. If the same thing is happening in Britain, America, Germany, Japan, and Australia— so ran the argument—it must be something beyond the control of man. There was even emulation, not to say envy, between nations and individual cities, as to the statistical measure of this frightful social failure. The pride of London suffered when its growth was outpaced by that of New York; France felt a loss of prestige when Berlin exceeded Paris; Birmingham and Glasgow watched each other's populations as two Forsytes watched each other's bank balances. To me all this seems as misguided as if cities were to boast of having the highest infant death-rate or incidence of tuberculosis.*

INTRODUCTION

In the last few years there has been a change. It is too much to claim that social thinkers and political leaders are as yet agreed upon a policy for controlling the size and distribution of towns, or as to the means by which it can be applied. But at least some are now awake to the subject. Though great harm has been done by the past indifference, there are still immense opportunities in the world for a better form of town development if a consensus of opinion can be created. In Great Britain, as I show in this book, a period of vast rebuilding lies ahead, and we have clearly-marked alternatives before us as to the principles of town structure and town distribution that should guide the rebuilding. The same is true in the United States. In Britain to a certain extent, and even more in the European and Asiatic countries where there has been great devastation, the replacement of war-damaged towns and parts of towns, to which governments must give financial aid and guidance, provides both the need and the opportunity for considered replanning, and for a radical change in the direction of town development.

In the many countries where industrialization has still to come there is an even greater opportunity; they can, if they will, profit by the mistakes of Great Britain as the classic land of the industrial revolution, and by a study of the line of thought by which we hope in some degree to correct these mistakes. The garden city idea, though hitherto misunderstood and disregarded at home, is one of Great Britain's major contributions to the pool of the world's thought. I restate it in this book in the belief that it is the key to the future pattern of town and country for industrial countries.

One of my purposes is to show that building new towns is not an evasion of the problem of making the best of existing towns, but is indispensable to the solution of that problem. In Great Britain and in other countries where the aggregation of population has gone too far and the central parts of large cities are therefore grossly congested, you simply cannot reconstruct the old cities on decent human standards without at the same time building new towns or extending the smaller towns; and in nearly every region you must do both the latter things.*

It is a secondary issue whether the new-town building shall be promoted separately as a means of drawing-off industry and population from great cities, leaving the latter to take advantage subse-

16

quently of the relief of pressure so brought about—which was
Ebenezer Howard's strategy—or whether the more open redevelopment of the large cities is to be consciously correlated with new-
town building—which is the strategy I myself prefer, and which
now seems to be emerging in Great Britain.

A secondary issue also is the degree in which the whole business
of town development demands public guidance, though it can
hardly be doubted that in all countries some public guidance is
essential. The methods will differ under different governmental
systems. In Britain we are moving towards a system in which the
work of town development and redevelopment is shared between
local authorities and private enterprise, under a state planning
control, exercising restriction here and encouragement there, but
not carrying this control to the point of dictation either to businesses or persons as to where they shall settle themselves. A more
collectivist country like Russia may use more compulsive methods.
A less collectivist country like the United States, while it cannot
wholly dispense with governmental planning restrictions, may
seek to rely more on a consensus of opinion among industrialists,
and on direct pressure by workers in industry on their employers,
possibly developing free-enterprise or co-operative agencies for
the creation of decentralized settlements.*

I have my own views as to the balance of governmental control
and private initiative that will most surely and satisfactorily produce a good town and country pattern. But I think the case for the
desirable pattern is in principle prior to and separate from the
problem of the methods by which it could be brought about. The
essential garden city idea is as applicable to Russia as to the
United States; as important to a Balkan or Asiatic state beginning
on the process of industrialization as to Great Britain seeking to
correct the worst consequences of industrialization. Howard's idea
of Social Cities as an alternative to continuous metropolitan spread
needs the consideration of New York and Moscow, Rio de Janeiro
and Peking, Melbourne and Brussels, no less urgently than of
London, Birmingham and Glasgow. I do not think it can be brought
about without some governmental control of land-use; but on the
other hand I do not think it can be done well without much participation by free enterprise. It is better however that the devising
of planning methods should spring out of socially-accepted aims.

INTRODUCTION

If we know the sort of towns we want, we shall be disposed, indeed we shall be impelled, to develop any governmental machinery necessary to produce them. It is on this principle that Britain is feeling its way towards the minimum and indispensable controls. We did not start with a craze for a planning machine and then look around for a job for the machine to do. That is why I think the British experience is worth study.

Another purpose I have had in this book is to direct attention to the fascinating human interest of town building as an enterprise in itself. To take part in the creation of a town *ab initio* is among the most exciting and enlightening experiences that can fall to the lot of man. I happen to be one of the very small group of people who have had this experience twice in modern England. There is unique pleasure and satisfaction in sharing in a great piece of physical constructive work, to see it shaping itself under your eyes as the result of thought and decision and labour. The permanence of the result is no small part of its attractiveness; you cannot but realize that the great fabric under construction is not only giving better surroundings to the thousands of people with whom you are associated in producing it, but will be the home and background of a community during ages to come. Of what other form of human activity is that true in the same direct and comprehensive sense?*

Not less enthralling is the social experience. In my chapter describing the social life of Letchworth and Welwyn I make an effort to see it from the point of view of inhabitants who settled in these towns only because they found work there and not because they were interested in the theories and purposes of the town-builders. For those who were so interested, the experience had another dimension. In the building of future new towns many people might enjoy this fuller experience if the adventure of town building seizes their imagination and becomes, as it well may, a widespread enthusiasm.

Especially would it interest men and women whose early years have been spent wholly in large cities and who are unacquainted therefore with the personal and social reactions of a 'community' in the sense of a local geographical group. Yet I have the best of personal reasons for realizing that these are just the persons whom it is most difficult to convince on this point. Before I became a citizen of small towns I was a saturated and unquestioning Londoner for twenty-five years. I was born in an apartment dwelling in inner London, and my family followed the normal progression by stages outwards to the suburbs. I lived in houses with yards and houses with gardens, and I went to school with the children of clerks and manual workers and grew up in familiarity with the different varieties of the London outlook and way of life. Then for a number of years I was engaged in the management of tenement dwellings and rows of cottages in the central and middle-ring districts, and this and other interests brought me into close contact with the life of workers in the East End and the southern and eastern proletarian suburbs. Thus I came to have a fair knowledge of ordinary workaday London life, and when the name 'London' is cited it is these vast areas of drab dwellings and the cramped lives of the millions of people therein that first spring to my mind.

But I also became in that period well acquainted with the infinitely smaller and entirely different London once summed up in the word 'Bloomsbury', with its vivid but unrooted cultural and intellectual life and its round of theatres, concerts, ballet, lectures, dancing, personal encounters, and discussion of politics and literature in coteries and cafés. It is a life with real charm for people adapted to it by curiosity, receptivity, and a particular range of interests. Most Londoners living that life to-day would respond contemptuously to the suggestion that there could be a richer interest, even any interest at all, in the life of a country town. It is hard to get them to see that it is possible to be right up to date in metropolitan art, manners, and thought, to feel a man of the age and thoroughly in the swim, and yet to be uneducated in some of the most fundamental things—to misapprehend the very nature of human society and of the world.

Nowadays when I revisit this 'Bloomsbury', where (such is the power of a misspent past) I still feel some intellectual consanguinity with the denizens, I find they on the other hand look on me as an ex-civilizee who owing to some flaw in his make-up has 'gone native'. They label me with some momentarily current term of abuse—a few years ago the word was 'escapist'—or quote G. K. Chesterton's description of a character in a story who 'went to live in a garden city like a man forgotten of God'. They are untouched by the retort that the commonest form of 'escapism' to-day is to seek to lose one's identity in a crowd; and they forget that Chesterton was more aware than any writer of his time of 'the anarchy and insane peril of our tall and toppling cities'. Despite many attempts I cannot make the bright spirits of Bloomsbury understand that an escaped Londoner is more awed by the gaps in their philosophy than by their acquaintance with the last six months' output of commercialized art. And even in this matter their treasured lead, unimportant as it seems to me, is being filched from them by the universality of radio.

It is not my wish however to provoke a mass migration from Bloomsbury. Though it is quite possible that the tendency of the urban intelligentsia to mental herd-impulses may at any moment make Ebenezer-Howardism a fashionable cult, I have confidence that (unlike the lemmings) they will leave plenty of time for the fashion to change again before taking action. For my part, if I have become too conscious that man does not live by theatres and art galleries alone, I do not forget that varieties of culture, including the metropolitan variety, have their value and must claim their priests and acolytes.

I shall be content if I convey to some by this book that they may find fulfilment, and highly pleasurable experiences, in pioneering new communities. I do not conceal that they may suffer shortages of comfort for a time, and shortages of some cultural amenities to which dwellers in great cities are accustomed. But I point to real, indeed priceless compensations, in addition to the advantage of good family homes in gracious surroundings. A wider circle of friends and companions, a sense of partnership in a great enterprise with permanent results, a deepened consciousness of community, a share in another kind of culture springing from voluntary activity and personal creativeness—these are among the dividends of investing one's life in community building. Only a minority can ever have the chance to do so, and for them it is no sacrifice. But it is not this minority alone that the partial migration from the overcrowded cities will benefit. Their departure will leave room in those cities for rebuilding them in a manner far more satisfactory for the great majority who will remain unmoved either emotionally, by arguments such as mine, or physically, by the dispersal policy to which those arguments point.

Finally, whether people agree with the proposals in this book or not, there will be an immense gain from a quickened interest in these great issues of the structure of towns and the interaction of town and country. Both in new towns and in old, the ordinary citizen might have, and when he realizes the possibilities will have, more influence on the shape of things to come. Town building and town rebuilding, though they require specialists of many different techniques, are not matters for technicians solely, or even primarily. Every resident and worker should be not only an interested critic of his town's development, but an active contributor thereto. Experience in the building of the two garden cities has impressed on me this fact above all others: that a town is not merely its fabric but its society. A town expresses the qualities, the purposes, and the inter-relationships of those who are conscious of and take part in its policy. At every stage the community influences the fabric and the fabric the community. Especially in a living democracy, where there is some social guidance informed by common ideas, but much scope is left for spontaneous group activity and personal initiative, town building is one of the most inspiring of social adventures.

Welwyn Garden City
July 1945

Addendum

As I correct the proofs of this book there comes the welcome announcement that the Minister of Town and Country Planning and the Secretary of State for Scotland have appointed a New Towns Committee with the following terms of reference:

'To consider the general questions of the establishment, development, organization and administration that will arise in the promotion of New Towns in furtherance of a policy of planned decentralization from congested urban areas; and in accordance therewith to suggest guiding principles on which such Towns should be established and developed as self-contained and balanced communities for work and living.'*

This takes into a new phase the development of British planning

INTRODUCTION

policy discussed in Chapters II and VII of this book. The long
period of debate seems to be drawing to its close, and the period
of action to be setting in.

October 1945.

PART ONE

THE GARDEN CITY MOVEMENT
A REVALUATION

'Human beings, in their present condition, may be likened to bees in the act of swarming, as we see them clinging in a mass to a single bough. Their position is a temporary one, and must inevitably be changed. They must rise and find themselves a new abode. Every bee knows this, and is eager to shift its own position, as well as that of others, but not one of them will do so till the whole swarm rises. The swarm cannot rise, because one bee clings to the other and prevents it from separating itself from the swarm, and so they all continue to hang. Indeed, there would be no outlet for the bees if each one were not a living creature possessed of a pair of wings. . . . If among these bees who are able to fly not one could be found willing to start, the swarm would never change its position. And it is the same among men.'—TOLSTOY, *The Kingdom of God is within You.*

In his book *To-morrow*, published in 1898, Ebenezer Howard quoted this passage from Tolstoy. It was one of the quotations omitted when the book was reissued in 1902 as *Garden Cities of To-morrow*, and which in the new edition[1] I have restored; because they are clues to influences on Howard, and time has made them even more apposite to his proposals. Tolstoy's words, of course, referred to the moral rather than the physical swarming of mankind. Yet how relevant they are to the urban problem and to the movement Howard created!

Howard's place in history is that, among the living creatures clinging to the mass and possessed of spiritual wings, he was the one prepared to start the flight. But though he took off in 1904 with the foundation of Letchworth, the swarm is still there, and a general movement to change position is only just becoming visible.

[1] Faber & Faber, 1946.

Anyone who has watched the swarming of bees knows that it is a long and devious process. Individual bees fly in all directions, joining, leaving and rejoining the swarm many times; and for a while it is difficult to tell whether they are in a phase of agglomeration or of decongestion and dispersal. But if you wait patiently, in time the ball begins to get smaller and you see the process of relocation under way.

Howard, starting the movement, had a clear idea of where to go. Other mobile bees, unsettled by his lead, were not so clear, and for years the air of the town planning movement was full of their buzzings to and fro and round about. If you read the planning literature of the forty-two years between *Garden Cities of Tomorrow* and the *Greater London Plan 1944* you cannot wonder at the time it has taken for the urban swarm to show a definite new direction of movement.*

It is unmanly to mourn the lost years, useless to cry over spilt suburbs. Now that a new direction of movement is at last visible it is, as I shall show, the one indicated by the pioneer bee, Howard. We may gain in unity and speed by reminding ourselves of the lead he gave.

Chapter I

EBENEZER HOWARD AND THE GARDEN CITY IDEA

The Problem of Urban Aggregation

Aclassic is always more respected than read, except by a few specialists. The singular fate of *Garden Cities of To-morrow* is that, since the first year or two after its publication, it has been left unread even by specialists. Evidence of this is the almost universal misuse of the term 'garden city'. No one who reads the book could possibly misunderstand what Howard meant by the term; yet among those who employ it in an entirely different and wrong sense are all but a few of the planning writers known to the public. Such a state of affairs exists in the literature of no other science, art or technique. It is queer enough that exponents of planning should not have read the book. Why they should affect to know what is in it without reading it I cannot explain.

More explicable is the neglect of the book and its thesis in academic circles, notably those of sociology and economics. It is not read in those circles because it is too easy to read. Because no one needs a wet towel around his head to grapple with it, it does not seem a serious contribution to thought. It has been disregarded as a mere popularization. But in fact its analysis is original, shrewd, and sound, and its proposals are realistic and important. It was sheer bad luck that Howard had no follower who could clothe his creative ideas in the difficult language that trained minds understand. Having made some effort to acquire this technique—though clarity keeps breaking in—I attempt in this chapter to summarize Howard's argument and proposals in the light of the modern approach to the urban problem.

He begins by assuming agreement that the herding of the people in large and crowded cities is bad; and by giving some telling quotations from well-known men as a reminder of the strength of feeling on this matter.

No one would have questioned this in 1898; not one person in a thousand would question it now. But a writer of to-day, wanting to be taken seriously, would not assume the undesirability of urban aggregation or high density of population, nor even the facts. He would begin by statistics establishing the degree of aggregation and density, and trends over a period. He would then analyse the factors in human satisfaction, or in economic efficiency, and show that aggregation and high density have on balance an effect on total satisfaction or efficiency, and perhaps, by graphs, that an adverse effect is correlated with the degree of aggregation or density. Nor could he stop there. He would have to anticipate and meet in advance every conceivable comeback of sceptical ingenuity or wishful thinking, as for example a possible line of thought suggesting a correlation between agglomeration-plus-density and the tempo or intensity of communal life. He might support his thesis by a piece of research into the relative mental and cultural intensity of life in a slice of Birmingham at 200 persons per acre and in Boar's Hill, Oxford, at ten persons per acre. And so on. Without doubt such researches have influence when they confirm the less formally arrived-at judgments of the reader. They also have a usefully paralysing effect on people prone to creative action on incomplete data; to put it less favourably, they can be a defensive mechanism for those who dislike decision. Without in any way deprecating research in fields of uncertainty, I think this assumption of Howard's is so obviously true that his omission of proof of it is no demerit.

Howard then goes on to state the problem as he sees it: 'How to restore the people to the land—that beautiful land of ours, with its canopy of sky, the air that blows upon it, the sun that warms it, the rain and dew that moisten it—the very embodiment of Divine love for man.' Here again Howard's assumptions are those of urban humanity at large; they have been confirmed, perhaps pathetically but beyond dispute, by the success of the suburban builder. Virtually every city dweller in treeless streets and garden-less houses longs to escape from them, and those who cannot envy those who can.

Next Howard analyses briefly why the people had come to be aggregated in huge cities. And though his language is simple, his analysis seizes on the essential causes. Contrasting the attractions of town and country, he gives to the 'Town Magnet' first the pull of opportunities for work and high wages (though the high wages are offset by high living costs), next of social opportunities and amusements, and last of well-lit streets. (Note that he puts wages and work before the 'cultural' attractions; many eccentricities of policy derive from reversing this order in the analysis.) The pull of the 'Country Magnet' is in natural beauty, fresh air, healthfulness. The disadvantages of Town are distance from work, the 'isolation of crowds', sunlessness and dirty air, and the slums. Those of the Country are dullness, lack of society, low wages, lack of amusements, general decay.

If anything Howard loads the dice against the country as a place to live in. He was a townsman, and though in his scheme he shows full understanding of the importance of agriculture and the rural way of life, it is easy to see that he has no hankering after a country life himself, and assumes (correctly I am sure) that the majority of British people are like him in this respect. When therefore he finds the solution in a combination of the advantages of Town and Country—the 'Town-Country Magnet'—he proposes a Town in the Country, and having within it the amenities of natural beauty, fresh air and healthfulness. He does not propose a mixture of Town and Country, though he has been accused of that by writers who have not read his book.*

A New Conception of the Town

At the head of Chapter I (1902 edition), Howard cites this passage from Ruskin's *Sesame and Lilies*:

'Thorough sanitary and remedial action in the houses that we have; and then the building of more; strongly, beautifully, and in groups of limited extent; kept in proportion to their streams and walled round, so that there may be no festering and wretched suburb anywhere, but clean and busy street within and the open country without; with a belt of beautiful garden and orchard round the walls, so that from any part of the city perfectly fresh air and grass and sight of far horizon might be reachable in a few minutes' walk. This the final aim.'

Howard had probably not noticed this passage before writing his book, but (except for the wall) Ruskin's picture of the ideal town is very close to Howard's physical conception.[1] It is what he means by the Marriage of Town and Country.

The famous diagram of the Garden City is familiar to many who have not seen Howard's book. It was a diagram only, and intended, in Howard's words, to be 'merely suggestive'. But the essence of it is a defined and rather compact town, of about 1,000 acres, or say one and a half miles diameter, near the middle of a site of 6,000 acres, 5,000 of which are permanently dedicated to agriculture. Such importance was attached by him to the limitation of the size of the town, and the reservation of the surrounding land for agriculture, that the whole 6,000 acres was to be in the same ownership; no outside interest must be able to exploit the fringe land for suburban development. And it was fundamental to Howard's conception that when the population grew to fill the prescribed urban area, further development should jump right over the sacrosanct agricultural belt and another town should be started, with its own green belt similarly protected. No previous writer (except perhaps More) was so clear and definite about the permanent delimitation of Town and Country zones.[2]

Within the town functional zoning is basic. Howard's Garden City is to be industrial and commercial, with a balanced mixture of all social groups and levels of income. Areas are worked out for the zones; public buildings and places of entertainment are placed centrally, shops intermediately, factories on the edge with the railway and sidings. Houses are of different sizes, but all have gardens, and all are within easy reach of factories, shops, schools, cultural centres, and the open country. Of special interest is the central park and the inner Green Belt, or Ring Park, 420 feet wide, containing the main schools, with large playgrounds, and such buildings as churches.

Howard never claimed that his areas and densities were more than a provisional estimate. But they were based on a pretty sound assessment, on the standards of the time, of the likely balance of needs. The population suggested was 30,000 within the town, giving an overall density of 30 persons per acre; and 2,000 in the country belt, or 2 persons per 5 acres.

[1] Ruskin's ideal is *oppidum in agris*. For a beautiful description of a town of this type (Avila, in Spain) see George Santayana's *Persons and Places* (1944).
[2] See Appendix I.

The maximum housing density, including access roads, works out at 80 persons in about 14½ houses per acre, the size of family assumed being 5½. The same number of dwellings, at a present-day average of 3½ persons per family, would bring Howard's maximum housing density to 51, his overall town density to 19, and his total town population to 19,000 on the 1,000 acres. In the 47 years since 1898 space requirements for nearly all town purposes have risen; and popular housing standards have greatly advanced. Howard's space standards have proved somewhat too low; but at least he can be acquitted of being an advocate of 'sprawl and scatter'.

The layout of the town was to be planned in advance, and its development controlled by leases limiting the use of sites to their appropriate purposes. Building and architectural controls were to be applied, but Howard is insistent on variety, freedom for individual taste, as well as order. The planning is conceived as a teamwork of many minds—'of engineers, architects, artists, medical men, experts in sanitation, landscape gardeners, agricultural experts, surveyors, builders, manufacturers, merchants, financiers, organizers of trade unions and co-operative societies.' But 'there should be unity of design and purpose':*

'A town, like a flower, or a tree, or an animal, should, at each stage of its growth, possess unity, symmetry, completeness, and the effect of growth should never be to destroy that unity, but to give it greater purpose, nor to mar that symmetry, but to make it more symmetrical.'

In detail the 'houses and groups of houses' display 'very varied architecture and design', and some have 'common gardens'; and there is insistence on 'general observance of street line or harmonious departure from it'. It is to be noted that Howard had no nostalgia for the past. He was a true Victorian, a child of Macaulay, an almost uncritical believer in progress. Everything in his town was to be the very latest thing; all further developments of science were to be allowed for, and adopted as they came along. He was perfectly sure that further Garden Cities would be as great an advance on his own ideas as these were on the towns of the past.

At times I do not share this certainty. Even less would it be shared by the Georgian Group, or the Society for the Protection

of Ancient Buildings. But Howard was much more representative
of the vast majority of the British people, then and to-day, than
we who, doubting our own age's ability to build beautifully, feel
we must coddle the decayed relics of a past age of taste. Whether
we are right or wrong, Howard had no such despair. For him the
world's great age began anew all the time.

This is not to say he was without aesthetic appreciation. Here
again he was closer to the majority than to the *élite*. He loved
flowers, trees, animals, children, healthy and comely people. And
though he knew perfectly well that others discerned beauty in the
shapes, colours and historical associations of buildings, and
allowed for this in his scheme, as he allowed for all interests, I
think he himself judged the beauty of a house by its aura of human
habitability and comfort and the garden leading up to it, its relation to a setting of trees and shrubs, rather than by its lines or
masses or fidelity to some architectural tradition. In this he was a
representative man, sharing the common feeling. It is a thing that
planners and architects should never forget. In seeking to spread
their own taste, they must meet in the gate the different, perhaps
more primitive, but not less passionate taste already possessed by
ordinary folk.

A feature of Howard's town plan was its division into neighbourhoods, each based on the population required for one school, and
having its community sub-centre.

'Each ward, or one-sixth of the city' (with about 5,000 population) 'should be in some sense a complete town by itself, and thus
the school buildings might serve, in the earlier stages, not only as
schools, but as places for religious worship, for concerts, for
libraries, and for meetings of various kinds. . . . Work, too, would
be practically completed in one area before commencing on
another.'

Another feature was the limitation of the number of shops, in
the interest both of a better service and of a higher ground rent
revenue. Howard evolved an ingenious system for 'local option',
by which the admission of further shops could be authorized by
popular vote, giving the existing shopkeepers a strong incentive to
satisfy their customers. The principle was to be that of competition
on a basis giving enough turnover for a trader's livelihood, the
public authority and co-operative societies joining in the competi-

tion; and it is a principle worth study by those who see and do not like the final logic of the present trend towards monopoly in universal state ownership.

But Howard did not believe in 'local option' in the commoner sense of a vote to bar public-houses. He wanted their number controlled, and their character regulated on the lines that have since become generally accepted.

Integral to Howard's scheme was a system of quasi-public land ownership, which is of no less importance than his physical pattern. It must be remembered that he wrote at a time when Land Reform movements were prominent in political discussion. Universal education had intensified the consciousness of the working masses of their 'exploitation'; innumerable books and speeches pointed out the contrast between the riches of the few and the poverty of the many. The clearest, most obvious, case of unearned wealth was that derived from land in great cities, which anyone could see multiplied in value without any action by the owners. Many people, whose prophet was Henry George, held that the land monopoly was the root of all inequality, and that if land rent were appropriated for the public the economic system would in other respects work automatically to the advantage of all. And though the rising socialist movements did not agree with this, they certainly agreed that land rent was socially an injustice, and on this one point they had common ground with the more radical section of the then powerful Liberal Party.

Howard's scheme was offered as a solution of the problem of land rent as well as of the problem of city congestion, which were obviously inter-tangled. His proposal that the site of any new town, including its country belt, should be in one ownership, and that profit on the land development should be limited to a normal commercial return, was intended as a means for securing land rent, due to the increase of population, for the community. Much of his book is devoted to this financial aspect of the scheme; and it is well done; the figures are out of date, of course, but the arithmetic is sound. Land values increase as a town grows, and Howard's method of leasehold control remains the best way to secure for the public the surplus value over cost of development in a new town.*

As regards the values in the large cities from which industry and

31

population were to be dispersed, Howard's forecasts are grim. The outward movement would cause such a fall in values that the owners, to avoid total loss, would come to terms with the public, so that the old centres could be rebuilt at far lower density. As the excess population would be drawn off by independent effort elsewhere, and not pushed out by planning regulations, compensation would not arise; any more than it does in an American city when private development in the suburbs renders central districts derelict.

This disposal of vested interests by a 'strategy of indirect approach' may seem nowadays somewhat ruthless, though it seemed less so in the atmosphere of the Land Reform controversies of the 1890's. In those days there was no surtax; no 50 per cent death duty. Since then much proletarian bitterness has evaporated under the balmy breezes of graduated taxation. And yet I am not at all sure that the blindness of the urban landowners, their unwillingness to meet planning half-way, may not bring about the uncompensated fall in central values which Howard forecast. A dispersal policy is beginning in advance of a settlement of the compensation and betterment problem; and it is likely that it may take the form of the drawing-off of congestion by positive development outside, as Howard proposed, to a greater extent than by the imposition within the cities of lower density standards involving compensation to landowners.[1]*

The 'Unique Combination of Proposals'

Let me now set out the main components of Howard's Garden City idea:

1. *Planned Dispersal:* The organized outward migration of industries and people to towns of sufficient size to provide the services, variety of occupations, and level of culture needed by a balanced cross-section of modern society.

2. *Limit of Town-size:* The growth of towns to be limited, in order that their inhabitants may live near work, shops, social centres, and each other, and also near open country.

3. *Amenities:* The internal texture of towns to be open enough

---

[1] If this is the shape of things to come, the Uthwatt Report, instead of being dreaded as a torpedo, ought to have been welcomed as a raft for the urban landowners.*

to permit of houses with private gardens, adequate space for schools and other functional purposes, and pleasant parks and parkways.

4. *Town and Country Relationship:* The town area to be defined, and a large area around it reserved permanently for agriculture; thus enabling the farm people to be assured of a nearby market and cultural centre, and the town people to have the benefit of a country situation.

5. *Planning Control:* Pre-planning of the whole town framework, including the road-scheme, and functional zoning; the fixing of maximum densities; the control of building as to quality and design, but allowing for individual variety; skilful planting and landscape gardening design.

6. *Neighbourhoods:* The town to be divided into wards, each to some extent a developmental and social entity.*

7. *Unified Landownership:* The whole site, including the agricultural zone, to be under quasi-public or trust ownership; making possible planning control through leasehold covenants, and securing the social element in land value for the community.

8. *Municipal and Co-operative Enterprise:* Progressive experimentation in new forms of social enterprise in certain fields, without abandoning a general individual freedom in industry and trade.

Howard, always a modest man, made no exaggerated claim for his idea. He called it a 'unique combination of proposals'. For the principle of organized outward migration he gave credit to Edward Gibbon Wakefield and Professor Alfred Marshall; for the system of quasi-public land tenure to Thomas Spence and Herbert Spencer; and for the conception of a model town in an agricultural estate to James Silk Buckingham.

Actually all these credits are too selective. Each of the writers named was one in a long line of people developing the ideas in his particular field. Each made some contribution, and each is of importance to the subject of this book as a link in some chain of influence on Howard. But the three components which Howard consciously combined really go much further back in history; and if it were vital (which it is not) to hand out graded bouquets some of the largest ought to go to Moses, Ezekiel, Plato, Aristotle, Sir Thomas More, and Robert Owen.[1]

[1] I have attempted in Appendix I to trace briefly the historical anticipations of Howard's concept of a country belt permanently reserved against town expansion.

THE GARDEN CITY MOVEMENT: A REVALUATION

It is a new combination of elements, however, that distinguishes any great invention. And, as my list shows, Howard combined many more elements than the three he names.

He included, for example, the idea, then relatively new, of providing family houses with gardens for industrial workers as well as for the better-off, which had in the preceding decade inspired a few great English industrialists (notably, Lord Leverhulme and George Cadbury) to bring to people of the lowest income the homely human standards of the architectural school led by Philip Webb, Norman Shaw and C. F. A. Voysey. He absorbed (I do not understand how) the hardly-emerged town planning principles of functional zoning, prescription of maximum density, and control of design, and incorporated them in his scheme; detecting, as no one else had done so clearly, the possibility of applying them to the planning of whole towns under a leasehold system. He reinvented the neighbourhood-unit idea, which is to be found in More's Utopia, and is implied in our system of local-government wards, but had been forgotten by townsmen. He adopted landscape gardening as an essential part of town design, whereas in his time people thought of it solely as a country art. He extended to town and housing development the fruitful idea of consumers' co-operation, which at the time was competing politically with the ideas of logical state socialism and of unrestrained private enterprise. And with all these things he combined the extremely important idea of the economic development of agriculture, partly on a freely co-operative basis, in relationship with a nearby town market.*

What is even more important, he steered his way with amazingly shrewd judgment between ideological extremes, detecting where social control was essential, and where individual freedom could be left free play. This marks him off from the communistic Utopians like Owen and Fourier. In Howard's garden city the land is owned by the community or an organization morally responsible to the community. But within a few necessary limitations, to safeguard planning, an industrialist carries on his factory with full freedom; a shopkeeper trades on his own account. The town is in a physical ring fence; but it is in no sense in an economic ring fence. At the same time, experiments in co-operative, municipal, and semi-municipal enterprise were to go on—as in fact they have gone on since in this country, and on very much the lines Howard foresaw or proposed.

Howard's economic set-up is now so obviously the right one, that newcomers to economic and political controversy may wonder that I comment on it at all. But to conservative minds in 1898 it seemed quite impossibly revolutionary; and to idealist minds it seemed a series of illogical compromises. It required much judgment, and at the same time much mental daring, to propose a scheme at once so novel and so practicable.

This I think is the really unique thing about Howard's scheme —the quality that caused it alone, of hundreds of imaginative descriptions of desirable communities, to issue in successful action. Previous literary pictures of ideal towns fall into two classes: those, like Plato's and More's, which were comprehensive and statesmanlike, and took full account of the complexities of society, but were meant only as 'patterns laid up in heaven', guides to urban policy generally; and those, like Owen's and Buckingham's, which were meant to be acted on, but showed a limited understanding of human nature and of economic and social requirements.

Howard's was, no less than Owen's and Buckingham's, a proposition for immediate action; but he was not thinking as a philanthropist of an underprivileged class, nor as a revolutionist of testing a novel social theory. His approach was rather that of an inventor of a type of new town suited to the conditions of the age, and meeting the wants of all classes and interests in the light of current knowledge and technique. He was an idealist in the sense in which an engineer conceiving and wanting to try out a better sort of bridge is an idealist; it would be better to call him a creative realist. His proposition did not imply (as Owen's did) a new conception of morals or behaviour or social relationships; he took people as he knew them, in all their variety, while allowing for such trends as were already discernible.

Seeing that cities as they stood no longer met the needs of modern society, were in fact out of date, Howard proposed to build new cities suited to the time, proceeding on the inventor's usual method of development by models and experiment. His unique triumph as an inventor in this new field is that when he got his models constructed, they worked.

Chapter II

THE BATTLE OF MODERN PLANNING THOUGHT

The Idea Submerged

The practical outcome of Howard's book is dealt with in the second part of this book, where I describe the methods by which the two garden cities in England were built, and examine their main features. Letchworth was started in 1904, Welwyn Garden City in 1920, each embodying Howard's principles. Both are primarily manufacturing towns, employing on the spot the bulk of their working inhabitants. Both are now firmly established and are centres of many prosperous industries and businesses. Between them they provide homes, workplaces and community life for nearly 40,000 people. They are as yet not quite half-way to their planned maximum populations; but already they demonstrate the merits of the garden city as a new type of town. And of course they have conclusively proved the widely doubted proposition that the foundation of entirely new towns is practicable in a long-settled country. They have proved also that the creation of towns which in their main physical features are completely planned through unified landownership is possible under a predominantly free-enterprise system.*

These remarkable British achievements are little appreciated in their own country. Howard and his associates made one propagandist mistake in siting Letchworth and Welwyn—building them in England within an hour's journey of London. One should have been built on some remote island like Mauritius, and the other in the Soviet Republic of Uzbuzchakistan. Planners and journalists would then have visited them and written them up, and we should have had lots of illuminating books on them. Also we should be excited about them as wonderful achievements, and be wanting to know why we can't have new towns of the same type in Dear Old Stick-in-the-Mud England.

Why have we only two garden cities up to now? The reasons are complex, but, frankly, I think the town planners and the allied architectural and amenity movements cannot escape some of the blame.

Tremendous consistency over a long period is required to lodge an idea in the public mind. Words and terms get misused unless we continually state what we mean by them. The writers and speakers who have sought to lead opinion on town and country planning have not been sufficiently precise or persistent in showing the public that the garden city idea is the major key for unlocking the problems of congestion and sprawl.

To understand what went wrong, recall the time-coincidence of Howard's book (1898) with the Locomotive Act (1896) and the beginnings of electric traction. Two new kinds of motive force, enabling people to live at great distances from work, hit the world at much the same time. Anyone who knows the history of towns and of housing—almost anywhere in the world except in very high latitudes—will realize that people working in towns have always wanted for their dwellings the amenities of both town and country; and that the carriage-folk, sometimes a small, sometimes quite a large class, have always obtained these combined amenities. Unless the town was open enough—as Athens was, or Roman-British Silchester, or More's ideal town—for houses with large gardens right inside it, invariably the carriage-folk placed their houses, in the classic phrase, 'between town and country', that is in what we now call suburbs.

It is so obviously the sensible thing, from a personal point of view, to make the best of both worlds, to 'marry town and country' for yourself in this way, that as a phenomenon of all history it needs no explanation. Literature is rich in illustrations of this tropism of the prosperous. Susanna's affair with the Elders occurred in her husband's lavishly planted suburban garden. Gibbon describes how, in the Rome of Caracalla and Geta (A.D. 211), 'the opulent senators had almost surrounded the city with their extensive gardens and suburban palaces'. And Keble Howard's *Smiths of Surbiton* was only one of the most popular of hundreds of modern novels idealizing this age-old trend. Nor has advice ever been lacking to those who could afford it to site their homes in large gardens in suburbs: I need only instance the precepts of Pliny the Younger, of the architect Alberti in fifteenth-century Florence, of the Elizabethan Stow, and of the Victorian Gilbert Scott.

What did the internal combustion engine and the electric motor do but vastly enlarge the noble company of carriage-folk? The tram, the bus, the train, the tube, enabled millions to seek the eternally desired situation between town and country. And the history of town development since 1900 is in the main the working out of that theme.

Howard and the industrialists who founded Letchworth with him saw clearly that the new motive powers would permit the personal desire for 'Town-Country' amenities and the needs of industry to be reconciled in a totally different way: the garden city way; which limited the size of towns, brought the 'natural' atmosphere within them, and used electricity for driving factories, and petrol engines for transporting goods, rather than both for shuttling human beings back and forth.

But the advocates of the garden city were overwhelmed by the new suburban rush. To a certain extent, I think, this was inevitable. There was no machinery for national planning, no prospect of state initiative in starting new urban centres, and it was bound to have taken time to educate opinion as to the true significance of these events or as to the alternative. The Locomotive Act had a start of two years on Howard, and I think, whatever efforts had been made, the new proletarian villas would for a time have outpaced garden city development.

As I have mentioned already, the evolution of the modern family house and open layout is a thread of events independent of the evolution of the garden city idea. Port Sunlight (1888) and Bournville (1895) played a leading role in popularizing the type and in associating it with advanced ideas of factory design. But, as it chanced, Letchworth played a still larger part, because there the new standards were applied on a whole-town scale; and there it was also that Raymond Unwin crystallized and codified the standards. Unwin's is a cardinal name in planning and housing history, because he combined three distinguished qualities—proficiency as a technician, sociological insight, and the ability to explain. Parker and Unwin's plan for Letchworth, which adapted Howard's schematic and quantitative diagram to the site conditions, was as great a contribution to planning technique as

Unwin's formulation of the maximum density code of twelve houses per acre was to housing technique; but in the circumstances of the next forty years the latter got far greater attention.[1]

Letchworth, the foundation of which roused for a time great interest in Howard's idea, had thrust upon it more even than it deserved of credit for the new housing standards. They became known as 'Garden City housing'—in itself a matter for pride. Unfortunately the public, hailing the new standards with enthusiasm, and then as now able to visualize houses but not towns, identified the component with the total product.

Everywhere enterprising builders and developers branded their goods 'Garden City houses' and their groups of houses 'Garden Cities'. When Copartnership Tenants Limited 'rose with Ealing in its wings' it claimed that its suburban estates were planned on 'Garden City lines'. Big business resulted, but the new and open housing schemes were almost wholly on city fringes. Along with them went huge developments of transport and the continued expansion of industry and commerce in and near the centres of the great cities. The Garden City Association struggled against the tide; it never ceased to advocate the true gospel, though perhaps at times it was too ready to be flattered by the use of the garden city label for good forms of layout in situations contrary to the garden city idea. In any case, the mass of printed matter poured out by the suburban builders submerged the tiny flow from the Association. And so the big woolly public, at first much taken with Howard's idea and wishful to pursue the subject, got thoroughly muddled between garden cities and garden suburbs.

Confusion was worse confounded by planners and journalists who turned an honest penny by writing up the movement. Before heaven and history I rate these the real culprits, because they had every chance to know better. Among them were most of the foreign writers on housing and planning as well as of the English ones. They wrote of Howard without assimilating his book or the

---

[1] Mr. Lewis Mumford is inclined to criticize Unwin for some of the confusion between the garden city idea and the standards of open layout. That is not my view. Unwin's double role as a great planner and a great housing reformer, and his work at Hampstead Garden Suburb, certainly made it easy for superficial students to be confused; but he himself was a clear thinker and kept the issues distinct in his teaching. He it was, in fact, who produced the clarifying slogan for Howard's physical arrangement, 'Towns on a Background of Open Country'.

prospectus of Letchworth. They used the term 'Garden City' to cover any sort of open or planted housing development from Bedford Park to a block of flats in Frankfort.

When Welwyn was started (1920) the promoting group debated whether they should give it a new label to kill the confusion; deciding finally to stick to Howard's term and to redefine and rehabilitate his idea. On the whole I think they have succeeded, though it has taken twenty-five years. One reason for adherence to the name was the belief that the same fate would overtake any new term that could be invented if planning writers proved incurably fluffy. And experience with one variant tried out proved this. In its early publicity Welwyn Garden City was described as 'a Satellite Town for London'. This was the first business use of the term. In using it the company explained that it meant a detached town, dependent on local industry and girdled by a country belt, but having economic linkages with London. No sooner had they got it into currency than planning writers began to pervert it—the company's invention, be it noted, precisely defined, popularized by them at great expense—exactly as they had misused the term garden city. Writers in this year of grace glorify 'Satellite Towns' and curse 'Satellite Towns', seeming to mean in each case the thing the Welwyn group were against—industrial salients on the edges of great cities.[1] For such developments, whether you support or oppose them, it is easy to find a descriptive name: for example, 'Industrial Garden Suburb'. Why steal or maltreat another firm's trademark?

The Period of Confusion

I think the deliquescence of planning thought in the 1920's and 1930's was largely due to this lamentable laxity of terminology in the profession and the lay movement.[2] But there were deeper

[1] In fairness to these writers I must add that Graham Romeyn Taylor's *Satellite Cities: A Study of Industrial Suburbs* (New York 1915) could be cited in defence of this usage, since it had four years' priority over the Welwyn Statement. In the absence of academic standardization, confusion of *terms* is excusable. But confusion between different *ideas* is a controversial misdemeanour, if not a crime.

[2] In my introduction to the new edition of *Garden Cities of To-Morrow* I have proposed a standardization of some of the terms used in the discussion of this aspect of town and country planning. For convenience this note on terminology is quoted in Appendix II of this book.

causes too. The rush to the suburbs, the still wider diffusion of building facilitated by the new methods of transport, and the chaotic conditions produced by business developments in city centres as a corollary, stirred up a lot of different reactions in different groups of people. Statutory town planning was in being and finding its feet, and the numerous groups of people who became conscious of particular distasteful symptoms of the course of urban development began to look to town planning for help, without grasping the problem as a whole.

This part of the story is complicated, and I must telescope it. But as it is so recent, brief reminders may suffice.

Each separate defect of the prevailing form of city development called forth its separate group of reformers. Thus the shortage of parks and playing fields was the concern of a number of societies. The protecting of trees, footpaths, bird sanctuaries, and ancient monuments engaged others. The frequent overwhelming of attractive stretches of country produced the National Trust and agitations to save by purchase this and that 'beauty spot'. This piecemeal approach widened out to a campaign to save large tracts of countryside from the builder, especially from 'ribbon development' and 'bungaloid growths'. And this touched off, and was reinforced by, a movement to keep free from building the land of highest fertility, in the interests of agriculture and the food supply. Under these combined influences the movement for rural preservation grew extremely influential, inspired a literature full of charm and admirable vituperation,[1] and enlisted the biggest parliamentary group interested in any issue to do with planning.

Parallel with these countryside movements there were many groups pressing for some control of design, in towns as well as in rural areas, their words of dread being the Petrol Pump, the Multiple Shop Fascia, and the Semi-Detached Bijou Palace. They did useful work in making the public more conscious of architecture, though they rather puzzled responsive laymen by the disposition of some of their architect members to tell them to execrate what others told them to admire.

Quite different groups of reformers were concerned about the

---

[1] *Britain and the Beast* (1937), edited by one of the wittiest writers and speakers on planning subjects, Mr. Clough Williams-Ellis, was perhaps the high spot of this literature.

sluggish pulse of the social life in the new housing estates, their lack of cultural facilities, their one-class make-up. This line of thought, again, extended itself to old built-up districts, and led to the enthusiasm for the Neighbourhood Unit—a mode of development which, though neglected when Howard proposed it in 1898, was much discussed in the United States before the last war and got to us later. Attention to this subject had practical results in the urbanization of the Village Institute, under the name of the Community Centre—a most paradoxical rebuke by the 'culturally starved' countryside to the assumed social maturity of the city.

Then the trend of industry to London and the West Midland cities, associated with the embarrassing growth of these agglomerations, produced a demand for Governmental encouragement of new industries in the Special Areas suffering from the decline of the heavy industries and consequent mass unemployment. As a result a number of industrial trading estates were built by governmental agencies in those areas, but as a detached activity, not related either to housing or the neighbourhood-unit line of thought.

I could go on to list other sectional movements of the inter-war Age of Chaos. But I will mention only one: the rehousing movement. The worst of the housing shortage was being overtaken, and it was realized that the task of the next period would be the rebuilding of the worn-out residential centres of the old cities, which had gone on decaying while the suburbs were being built and larger structures were replacing many central factories and commercial buildings. The pressure on space was so serious in the city centres, and land values so high, that luxury flats here and there replaced middle-class family houses, and municipalities began to return to a meaner form of the same expedient (which had been dropped when the new housing standards had come in) for slum-clearance rehousing. Every housing reformer with knowledge of the people's wants and ways of life deplored this reactionary lapse. But the journey between work and the suburbs had grown to an intolerable burden for the poorer workers, and there was evidence that some children in outlying housing schemes were being starved to pay Daddy's bus or tube fares.

Now the obvious answer to this dilemma between flat-dwelling and strap-hanging was Howard's: dispersal of work as well as of dwellings. It was the great chance for the planning movement to reassert the principles on which in its early days its leaders had been clear.

Instead of that the British public, just when it was beginning to take an interest in town planning, was bewildered by a prolific crop of academic fantasies. Flats, which in the days of sanity were looked on as a miserable makeshift for the family dwelling—a necessary evil by those who did not believe in bold town planning, and an unnecessary evil by those who did—were suddenly idealized by ardent but inexperienced young architects as a new and better way of life. Vienna became the beacon, and a misguided effort was made to evade the problem of land values and dispersal by substituting for the ideal of the private family house the quite illusory ideal of a communalized home life with a luxurious apparatus of crèches, nursery schools, common laundries, restaurants, workrooms, clubrooms and what-not.

Hitlerism in Europe caused a flight of architects to Great Britain, and in the London coteries who evolved these Babylonian theories there was more than a sprinkling of the type whom Mr. Robert Moses, Parks Commissioner of New York, has called 'Beiunskis'. Britain, like the United States, has benefited by many waves of continental technicians, and it would be to the loss of both countries if they cultivated an anti-Beiunski prejudice.[1] All the same these visitors mostly came from places where space standards are lower than ours, both in fact and aspiration; and newcomers to Britain could not easily understand the historic roots or the force of our democratic housing revolution. Some of these foreign friends, and the English architects fresh from school with whom they drank coffee, innocently misled each other.

The new architecture tried to strangle itself at birth by mixing its advocacy with half-baked sociological theories: mankind

[1] The term 'Beiunski' was derived by the ingenious Mr. Moses from the German expression 'bei uns' (with us), because, he said, these immigrant technicians were in the habit of reiterating: 'With us it was done this way.' Hundred-per-cent natives who may be tempted to exploit the term should first consider whether they themselves do not qualify for some of the Parks Commissioner's other amusingly abusive labels—'long-haired professors', 'vestal virgins', 'subsidized llamas', or 'starry-eyed dodos'. I am conscious that he would put me in this last class.

escaping the cramping bonds of the family, and so on. It shows the genuine vitality of this architecture that it survived this handicap.

Another coterie found its flag in the aristocratic planning of the eighteenth century, a period when the dominant class lived in detached country palaces and grand squares, but housed their retainers in tidy mews and rows of cottages—just as they dressed them in respectful uniforms. This school detested the informal layouts of a democracy which, having only one dwelling per family, wanted it to be their country house and town house as well. They had a case, but their carefully selected photographs of schemes designed by philistine council surveyors did not really prove that open layouts are inherently tasteless.

These purely visual enthusiasms all ignored consumer demand. Fortunately, as extremes, they cancelled each other out. Enthusiasts for the street were offset by Le Corbusier, who called it a 'gloomy canyon' and proposed to house the townsfolk all gloriously in towers of steel and glass. Space-cutting English architects who showed how you could crowd houses together at forty to sixty per acre were countered by the generous American, Frank Lloyd Wright, who showed how you could spread them out at one per acre. And these conflicting principles were exploited journalistically by the Sad Fog-Blowers and the Merry Dust-Throwers. They were all fun, but none met the social and economic conditions.*

During this period there was one moment of real peril for planning: when there was a temporary alliance between the extreme rural preservationists and the believers in rebuilding the cities at a high density by the use of multi-storied flats. Some fallen angel put into the minds of lovers of the country—men of culture and goodwill, and among the best of English society—the idea that their cherished fields and woods might be saved by continuing in this tidier form the site congestion of the cities. The Best corrupted is the Worst. This base temptation wormed its way into some of our noblest souls:

> We are the choice selected few;
> Let all the rest be damned;
> There's room enough in Hell for you;
> We won't have Heaven cramm'd.[1]

---

[1] Quoted in Begley's translation of *Nova Solyma* (1648).

In the end they told Satan to get behind them, but the thought lingered on long enough to colour one or two paragraphs of that enlightened document the Scott Report.*

Now it may be this welter of one-track thinking was inevitable as a phase in the evolution of opinion on this very complex subject. It must be remembered that the possibilities of town planning were being realized for the first time by fresh relays of people. Humanity always plays around with a new piece of apparatus as if it were a toy. But the public were confused by the obvious division of the planning forces. Planning had been identified in the first instance with the garden city idea, and now the garden city idea, which the public undoubtedly found attractive, was being abused by planners! It was exasperating to advocates of planned dispersal that they had to contend not only with the public's normal slowness in grasping any new idea, but with positive misrepresentations of their principles by writers on planning, some of whom were really in agreement with the garden city idea without knowing it. Howard's proposals were unmistakably clear. The two garden city companies had adopted these proposals and had stated them with equal clarity.[1] In building Letchworth and Welwyn they adhered closely to their intentions. It was inexcusable that writers on planning, and only less excusable that journalists, should have so persistently misconceived the aims of the garden cities and so ignorantly depreciated their achievements. Thereby wide circles of public opinion were led to believe that the garden city movement was to blame for suburban sprawl, for spoiling beautiful country, for indifference to architecture and beauty—in short, for the very things against which the movement was a revolt and a living protest.

If in those years of confusion the exponents of the garden city idea at times showed impatience with other planners, here is the explanation. As one of them, I disclaim any taste for acrimony in debate. Like Truthful James, I stand by the best Table Mountain manners:

> I hold it is not decent in a scientific gent
> To say another is an ass—at least to all intent;
> Nor should the individual who happens to be meant
> Reply by heaving rocks about to any great extent.

[1] I give extracts from early public statements of the two companies in Appendix III.

45

THE GARDEN CITY MOVEMENT: A REVALUATION

On a subject as many-sided as town and country planning, it is not to be expected that experts will all agree. But it is a responsibility of experts to be clear-minded, and to respect historical truth.

The New 'Symbiosis'

If the confusion to which I have referred has not yet been entirely removed, at any rate it is lessening. In recent years we have seen what biologists call a 'symbiosis' of these detached cells of thought on planning. A platform for unity was provided by the Planning Basis drafted by the Town and Country Planning Association in 1941[1] and endorsed by a number of other organizations, but it is difficult to judge how far the merging of opinion has been influenced by such efforts, or whether events would not have brought it about in any case. Nor does it matter. A set of common ideas and a practicable policy are being built up, and the outer public is at last beginning to understand the larger planning issues and the measures necessary to deal with them.

Governmental Commissions and Committees have helped in this. As long ago as 1920 the Unhealthy Areas Committee recommended the restriction of factories in London and the moving of industries to 'Garden Cities which should be founded in the country where the inhabitants will live close to their work under the best possible conditions'. There is little doubt that it was his chairmanship of this Committee that made Mr. Neville Chamberlain a believer in the garden city idea. This personal conversion of a future Prime Minister proved most important; for it was Mr. Chamberlain who set up the Barlow Royal Commission in 1937; a link often overlooked.

Between the Chamberlain and Barlow Reports, there came in 1934 the Marley Report, which endorsed the idea of 'Satellite Towns' in the exact sense given the term by the Welwyn group, and urged the building of more towns of that type, 'not in isolation but rather as elements in the wider sphere of regional and national planning'. And in 1936 came Sir Malcolm Stewart's

[1] The Association's analysis of the situation, and a fuller statement of the comprehensive policy it proposed, are to be found in the evidence it gave to the Barlow Royal Commission in 1938, and to the Scott Committee in 1942.

Report as Special Areas Commissioner, renewing the Chamberlain Committee's suggestion of a ban on new industries in London.

The Barlow Commission was the first body to take full evidence on the economic, technical, and sociological aspects of the urban problem. As a result its Report (1940) is the best official analysis of the problem. Also it made a great advance by its definite proposals for national planning, dispersal, and guidance of the location of industry. In fact the Report is the next great document in the case after *Garden Cities of To-Morrow*.

These were Government-printed reports, available to all. But up to 1941 they might as well have been written in Sanskrit for all their effect on the minds of the public or the sectional planners. What made this country planning-conscious was the bombing of our cities in 1940–1. This let in daylight in a double sense. People began to speculate on better things that might be built on the acres of rubble; and from this they went on to speculate how the out-of-date areas left unbombed might be replanned. It was just a lucky coincidence that when they first asked such questions, there was the Barlow Report, handy on the shelf, with the answer.

Now as soon as the common man and woman came into the planning discussion, common sense began to come in too. At first attempts were made, by architectural exhibitions based on ideas from the Period of Chaos, to sell them the fantasies. They showed, as all sane planners knew they would, a healthy sales resistance. A terrific storm blew up on Houses versus Flats, Terraces versus Semi-detached, Communal Living versus Family Privacy, and such things; and this led to a flood of questionnaires, brilliantly caricatured by Mr. George Formby in the film, 'He Snoops to Conquer'. If this flood did nothing else, it washed all the fantasies into the sea of oblivion.

Another result of the public taking a hand was good. Devotees of single interests—from rural preservationists to urban redevelopers, from antiquarians to bird-sanctuarians, from poster-haters to smoke-abaters, saw that to get anything done they must come to terms with each other.

Ideas on the land question began to emerge too. Councils who had to rebuild bombed towns, and amenity societies anxious to stop sprawl, found they had common ground in the necessity of legislation on compensation and betterment and the subdivision of ownerships, and of a policy for the placing of 'overspill'. The Uthwatt and Scott Committees sat and reported (1942). In the end, though not without differences of accent, a consensus of opinion grew up as to a pattern of town and country development that would best reconcile the various interests. With 'deliberate speed, majestic instancy', the Government ratified this consensus; accepting seriatim the principles of national planning, public land assembly, a compensation-betterment fund, decongestion of cities and dispersal of population and industry, and central guidance of factory location. Acts to implement some of these things are already passed; others are on the way.

Now what is the pattern that has emerged?

It is the garden city pattern: towns of limited size, of controlled density, on a background of safeguarded countryside; towns where people live near work, with planned industrial zones; towns which are real communities of all classes, fully equipped for social life; towns with gardens and open space; towns in which architectural control aims at harmony in diversity. And as means to these ends, unified landownership of large areas, with leasehold control to maintain good planning.

Of course we are still a long way from having achieved any of these aims. The war in Europe is only just over, and reconstruction has hardly begun. Not all the powers have yet been obtained, the organization is only in course of creation, and the trained personnel are too few. Many details remain to be worked out, and a great deal of further study and education is necessary both centrally and locally.

But some local and regional plans are at last being drawn on the new pattern. For a creative lead in this part of the task we owe much to Professor Sir Patrick Abercrombie. I rank the *Greater London Plan* 1944 with Howard's book and the Barlow Report as the third in the classic canon of planning. It is the first fully-worked-out 'garden city' plan for a great Metropolis.[1] The 1944

---

[1] I do not forget Raymond Unwin's Plan of 1929; but relatively that was no more than a sketch; Unwin was not given the backing or the resources for the detailed working out of the entirely sound principles his Plan enunciated and applied in broad terms.

Plan can of course be criticized in detail. But it comes close to meeting all the conditions: sociological, economic, technical, aesthetic. There is not one of the separate trains of thought I have listed (except the crazy ones) that it does not cater for and reconcile.

This 1944 Plan is a modern application of Howard's principle of Social Cities. Here is Howard's idea of what should happen when a city reaches its fixed population limit:

'How shall it grow? How shall it provide for the needs of those who will be attracted by its numerous advantages? Shall it build on the zone of agricultural land which is around it, and thus for ever destroy its right to be called a "Garden City?" Surely not. This disastrous result would indeed take place if the land around the town were, as is the land around our present cities, owned by private individuals anxious to make a profit out of it. For then, as the town filled up, the agricultural land would become "ripe" for building purposes, and the beauty and healthfulness of the town would be quickly destroyed. . . . The town *will* grow; but it will grow . . . by establishing . . . another city some little distance beyond its own zone of "country", so that the new town may have a zone of country of its own. . . . In course of time we should have a cluster of cities . . . so grouped around a Central City that each inhabitant of the whole group, though in one sense living in a small city, would be in reality living in, and would enjoy all the advantages of, a great and most beautiful city; and yet all the fresh delights of the country—field, hedgerow and woodland—not prim parks and gardens merely—would be within a very few minutes' walk or ride.'

Sir Patrick Abercrombie carries this idea of Social Cities back into the built-up part of London. He proposes to sort London out into a group of communities of defined size and population, bounded at least by park strips, main lines of communication, and other separating features, to which he gives the name 'perimeter barriers'. The same application of the Social Cities principle to old cities has been advocated recently by Mr. Lewis Mumford and Mr. Eliel Saarinen in the United States. Further, the Abercrombie Plan proposes dispersal not only to new towns, but also to existing country towns, which Howard does not mention in his book.

Both these extensions of Howard's idea were included by me in my restatement of his proposals (*New Towns After the War*) in 1918, written when I was in close association with him:

'If we were capable of a thoroughgoing application of [garden city] principles we should replan most of the old towns and disperse the vast town-tracts into federal groups of garden cities separated by agricultural belts; preserving all that is historic and beautiful in the more ancient central districts. All rebuilding should conform to new plans as the old houses wear out and leases fall in; and so the noble and healthy towns of the future would grow gradually out of the disorder of the present. Doubtless the necessity of making some sites revert to agricultural and park land would create difficulties about compensation and rateable value; difficulties which could hardly be surmounted unless the land first became public property. Even a partial replanning and a limitation of the number of houses per acre would, in default of that condition, present similar difficulties. But sooner or later this great problem must be faced if life is to be made worth living for the urban population.

'[Garden cities] may also give a lead for the revival of the existing country towns, many of which are possible centres for modern industry. . . . But in some cases their public services need to be brought up to date and their industrial equipment remodelled. . . . If the small towns could regain their vigour the development of a real national cultural life would be possible.'

I modified the former of these two passages in my 1942 edition. Even in the tentative way in which I expressed it I carried a good idea beyond the point which it is profitable to consider: an 'agricultural belt' around each London borough was not seriously in my thoughts. But in time some driving of separating green wedges and park belts through the congested central areas of London and other great cities may prove practicable if on further analysis it is held to be desirable. In the meantime the attractive 'poly-nucleation' proposed in the Abercrombie Plans is a difficult enough target to aim at.

The expansion of country towns with industries could however begin at once; and it is encouraging that many such towns, under the stimulus of the Country Towns Committee of the Town and Country Planning Association, have become alive to their chance under the dispersal policy.[1]*

We shall need both country town extensions and new towns. London on the lowest estimate must disperse over 1,000,000 people; Liverpool 250,000, Manchester 150,000, Leeds 50,000, Plymouth 40,000; and other cities large numbers. I think the housing standard demanded in practice will increase some of these figures; and that new developments of one kind or another will be needed for four to five million people. I doubt if as many as two millions can be added to existing country towns without overbalancing them. We shall want at least fifty new garden cities in Great Britain.*

In other countries, without doubt, the idea of controlled town expansion and new-town building will be adopted. Much of Europe has to be rebuilt; and in South-East Europe and Asia certainly, in South America, and probably (if on a smaller scale) even in Africa, many regions have their Industrial Revolution still ahead, and as they have to build hundreds, perhaps thousands, of towns, that distinguished British invention, the garden city, and our queer neglect of it, are likely to be the subject of vastly extended study. And many countries will be well advised to make much use of it.

What an opportunity this offers for technicians! From experience I can say that building a town is the most fascinating task it is possible to take part in. Some planners may feel dedicated to the not less important work of statutory control of land-use. Others may be drawn to municipal redevelopment inside the old cities. But many, I feel, ought to be attracted to the art and technique of building new towns—which, while closely linked with the other two jobs, will require its own specialized skill and produce its own rich reward in interest and satisfaction. Howard's two towns are there for study as prototypes, not for mere copying as stereotypes. He wisely wrote: 'Each generation should build to suit its own needs.' He never had the least doubt that the engineers, architects, surveyors, and landscape gardeners of his 'To-Morrow'—that is, of our To-Day—could build garden cities far superior to his experimental models.

Coming back to Tolstoy's bees, the swarm is on the move. The

[1] See *Country Towns in the Future England*, ed. S. Baron (Faber & Faber, 1944).

pioneers—the planners—now show a sense of direction, instead of buzzing into all quarters including the stratosphere, or nuzzling further into the swarm. If we can maintain unity, without scrapping our wings, we can lead the urban masses towards resettlement in healthier, happier, more productive and more gracious surroundings.

PART TWO

THE WORKING MODELS EXAMINED

'The time for the complete reconstruction of London . . . has not yet come. A simpler problem must first be solved. One small garden city must be built as a working model, and then a group of cities. . . . These tasks done, and done well, the reconstruction of London must inevitably follow. . . . Let us, therefore, first bend all our energies to the smaller of these tasks, thinking only of the larger tasks which lie beyond as incentives to a determined line of immediate action, and as a means of realizing the great value of little things if done in the right manner and in the right spirit.' —EBENEZER HOWARD, *To-Morrow* (1898).

In the context the 'London' of the above passage stands for our 'overcrowded, old-fashioned and effete cities', of which the Metropolis is cited as 'the largest and most unwieldy'. Howard founded both the Letchworth and Welwyn Garden Cities as experiments in and demonstrations of his thesis. They were intended to show the way to the redevelopment of great cities as groups of beautiful towns on a background of open country: a conception now informing the most advanced regional planning schemes. As successful working models they are of great importance and interest. I propose to describe in plain terms how they were built, some of the problems that were encountered in building them, and some of the lessons gained by this experience. The facts and figures I have sought to give accurately. The comments are necessarily personal, and though I endeavour to be dispassionate and fair, it must not be assumed that the companies and authorities responsible for the development of the two towns would agree with all I say.

The creation of entire towns is a very complex process, in which many agencies, public and private, share, and of which physical planning, land development, and town administration, though immensely important in shaping the character of a town (especially in the early years), are only a part. It will be understood, therefore, that in what follows I make no attempt at an exhaustive study of the process as exemplified at Letchworth and Welwyn. Within the fields, for example, of estate policy and local government I deal only with selected factors concerning which the experience at Letchworth and Welwyn seems likely to be interesting and to make some contribution to knowledge. Interlocked with the special questions that arise in the building of a new town are of course many matters that arise in the governance of any town, the undertaking of any piece of land development, the construction of any class of buildings, or the establishment of any urban service or organization of any kind anywhere. Even within the scope of the special experience of the two Garden Cities I am consciously selective. And I barely scratch the surface of the subjects of local government and estate management generally, on which massive and systematic text-books are available.

For convenience of reference I deal in parallel with each main aspect of development for both towns. It should be borne in mind throughout that the two towns, though distinguished from all other towns hitherto created by the combination of qualities devised by Howard, are very different each from each. The reasons for this are many: differences of topography, of regional situation, of the personalities taking part in their physical, social and cultural development (a surprisingly influential factor), and of the date of their foundation.

A gap of sixteen years separated the beginnings of the two towns. Letchworth was founded in 1904, when town planning was unknown in Great Britain, the idea of starting a town *de novo* was looked on as just madness, and pleasant planted surroundings for the urban masses seemed a Utopian dream. Welwyn Garden City was started in 1920, just after the first World War, when 'town planning' was in existence and feeling its way as a branch of government and was identified in the public mind with openness of layout, Lloyd George's slogan 'A fit country for heroes to live in' had caught the national imagination, and housing was being accepted for the first time as a public responsibility. But in 1920 the garden city idea was even less understood than in 1904. Both towns were the result of the enterprise and persistence of small groups of people who believed that the idea was sound, working against a background of general public indifference and with the minimum of official encouragement.

The principal data for the history of Letchworth and Welwyn are to be found in the archives and reports of the companies who developed them, in the minutes of their local authorities, in accounts written in various journals by persons who took part in their development, and in the newspapers published in the two towns. For some of the facts about the early history of Letchworth I am in debt to Mr. C. B. Purdom's *Building of Satellite Towns* (Dent 1925), and to officials of First Garden City Ltd. and of the Letchworth Urban District Council. In recalling the facts about Welwyn Garden City my own records and notes have been most usefully supplemented by information supplied by the directors and staff of Welwyn Garden City Limited. I am specially indebted, for reminders as to the history of Welwyn's finance and shopping policy, to Sir Theodore Chambers, K.B.E., Chairman of the company, and Capt. R. L. Reiss, its Deputy-chairman, both of whom for twenty-five years have not only carried much of the business responsibility for the town's development, but for most of the time have been residents in the town and have taken a great part in its public and social life.*

Chapter III

THE PHYSICAL PATTERN

Choice and Purchase of Sites

In the case of the First Garden City (Letchworth) the definite intention to build a town in demonstration of Howard's principles preceded the choice of a site. Howard formed the Garden City Association (now the Town and Country Planning Association) in 1899, and a period of propaganda followed, supporters being gradually gathered. Among these were Ralph Neville, K.C. (afterwards Mr. Justice Neville), who proved a leader of imagination and distinction, and gathered around him a group of energetic business and professional men. In 1902 a pioneer company set about examining possible sites. The qualities laid down as essential were: a freehold area of 4,000 to 6,000 acres in a 'ring fence'; nearness to a main railway and to London or some other large centre; and the practicability of water supply and drainage. A river or canal was thought desirable but not essential.

The promoting group found four fairly suitable sites (in Warwickshire, Staffordshire, Nottingham and Essex), and they nearly decided on the Chartley Estate in Staffordshire. On second thoughts they preferred the Letchworth Estate in Hertfordshire, a stretch of almost unbuilt-on land, 35 miles from King's Cross on the Hitchin-Cambridge branch of the G.N. Railway, and between 2 and 4 miles from the main line junction at Hitchin. The land being held by 15 owners, not all wishful to sell, great secrecy had to be maintained in the purchase negotiations. There were anxious moments; risks had to be taken by entering into some contracts before the whole purchase was assured. Finally (in 1903) 3,918 acres were bought for £155,587—£40 15s. per acre. Additional land was added at later dates, bringing the present estate to 4,574 acres, and the total price to £178,717.

In the case of the Second Garden City (Welwyn) it was the finding of a suitable site that prompted the initiation of the scheme.

56

Howard and three associates had previously noted the site, almost academically, as highly suitable for a new town, and it was by a sheer coincidence that it came into the market. The land was on both sides of the main London–York line of the G.N. (now the L.N.E.) Railway, 20 to 22 miles from King's Cross and 2 to 4 miles north of Hatfield, and at the junction of two branch railways. In 1919 part of this land (1,458 acres) was put up for auction, and Howard, after running round hurriedly to collect between £4,000 and £5,000 from a few friends, bought this area for £51,000. It was a daring, almost foolhardy, personal venture, for he had not enough money to pay the deposit of 10 per cent, and part of it had to be advanced by his agent on the day of sale.[1] The area bought at the auction, plus 230 acres of woodland on which an option had been obtained, was insufficient for a satisfactory scheme. By good fortune, the owner of much of the additional land necessary proved willing, though very reluctant, to sell it. Even so he and another adjoining owner would not sell the whole of the land the group wished to acquire, and the area purchased fell short of Howard's theoretical figure of 6,000 acres, and of what was really desirable for the provision of an adequate agricultural belt. In all the original estate came to 2,378 acres, the price of which, including timber and some buildings, was £105,804—£44 10s. per acre. Subsequent purchases have increased the estate to 3,411 acres. Further additions are likely to be made.

Thus both for Letchworth and Welwyn the choice of site was influenced, in fact determined, by the chance of a large area of suitable land being purchasable at one time. Difficulty and risk fell on the small groups of promoters in buying a sufficiently large and complete site. And in each case there was an element of luck in the success of the purchase. Secrecy was difficult, because technical surveys had to be made to ascertain that the intended town area was suitable for building, that water and drainage could be provided, and that other services could be made available. Yet full disclosure of the intentions, in the case of Letchworth, would have sent up the price of some of the indispensable parcels of land; and, in the case of Welwyn, would probably have led to the withdrawal of the land from the auction sale, owing to a tem-

---

[1] I described this incident in more detail in the preface to *New Towns After the War* (Dent, 1942).

porary wave of resentment among the 'county' residents at the very idea of an industrial town being established in their neighbourhood. I deal with the moral of all this in a later chapter.

The Garden City Companies

The bodies who acquired the sites and undertook the development of Letchworth and Welwyn were both public companies, registered under the Companies Acts, and inviting share capital from the public at large. In each case there was a pioneer company which, after the purchase of the site, conveyed it to a new company with a larger authorized capital.

First Garden City Ltd. was registered in September 1903 with an authorized capital of £300,000. Its structure was normal, except that dividends on its shares were limited to 5 per cent per annum cumulative, and any balance of profit had to be devoted 'to the benefit directly or indirectly of the town or its inhabitants'. This limitation, being in the Memorandum of Association, is not alterable except by consent of the High Court. The original directors were mostly successful business men—half of them successful industrialists—who, however, regarded their personal efforts for the scheme as work of public value. The Articles gave them the usual untrammelled powers of a commercial Board of Directors.*

Welwyn Garden City Ltd. was registered in April 1920 with an authorized capital of £250,000. In this case again the constitution was almost normal. The memorandum of Association imposed a limitation on dividends and an obligation to dispose of any balance of profit in the same way as at Letchworth. The dividend limit was expressed as 2 per cent above the yield of Government stocks at the time of subscription of shares, which, owing to the high return on gilt-edged securities at the time, brought the actual limit to 7 per cent (cumulative) instead of 5 per cent per annum. There was also a novel provision (this time in the Articles) for the appointment annually of three 'Civic Directors' by the local authority of the town, with the same powers as the other Directors. Both the limitation of dividend and the Civic Directors disappeared from the constitution of the Welwyn company in a reconstruction in 1934, to which I refer later. As at Letchworth, the

Directors of the Welwyn company were mostly business men, with one or two professional men. Three (including Ebenezer Howard, who remained on both Boards till his death in 1928) had had the advantage of experience in the development of Letchworth.

Both companies had for many years considerable difficulty in raising capital. The Letchworth company went to allotment on £40,000 subscribed by 'Directors and their relations'. At the end of the first year, despite much publicity, only £100,000 of shares had been subscribed; which figure should be compared with the £155,000 incurred in the purchase of the initial site. The Welwyn company raised in its first year £99,000, against £106,000 spent on the site and £16,000 on the expenses of the issue. Being thus starved of money for development, both companies had from the start to borrow, to the maximum amount possible, on mortgages on the land, and had to pay interest thereon, as well as administrative expenses, before any new revenue could be created. Both had to issue in their early years priority securities, such as mortgage debentures, and in the case of Welwyn, floated during the 1920 'boom', the interest rate was as high as 6½ per cent. Both therefore became, even for land companies, 'highly geared', and this tended to make the progressive raising of ordinary share capital increasingly difficult.

There is no doubt that the shortage of capital, due to public disbelief in the schemes, retarded development at times when it could have been profitably accelerated. This delayed the overtaking of interest on capital expenditure by revenue, and in turn intensified the disbelief of investors—the usual vicious circle of under-capitalization. On the other hand, chronic poverty induced habits of ingenuity and economy which enabled amazingly good value to be obtained for the money so parsimoniously doled out. But this was a mitigation only. On balance I am certain that the overall business results would have been more impressive had adequate capital been available and development say twice as rapid. With a little, not very much, more capital the two companies could have taken many opportunities they had to forgo. 'Jobbing backwards', it can be argued that the able business men responsible for Letchworth and Welwyn made a business mistake in proceeding with their schemes when they were not adequately backed by investors. If they had been governed by conventional business views on this matter, we should not have had the two garden cities.

Apart from dependence on a sceptical investment market, the method of development by public companies with a maximum dividend had immense advantages for schemes of this kind, which had social as well as business objects. The Directors, administering freehold estates, had no limiting Acts or Orders to bother them, no cautious civil servants to convince, no necessity to play up to pressure groups to avoid electoral defeat. On the other hand they were not heavy personal investors in the schemes; and while they acted with due responsibility as trustees for the capital subscribed, they showed no tendency to exploit unduly their land monopoly or to forget the public aims. Whether this would always be so in private enterprise companies working under a profit limitation it is possible to doubt. In these two cases the balance was in fact fairly held.

First Stages: Survey and Plan

Town planning, as experience has shown, can be a dismal art when the planners do not know what sort of town they want to produce. They tend to rely on research and surveys to make up their minds for them; but research and surveys only tell you what things are; not what they ought to be. The founders of Letchworth and Welwyn were fortunate in being agreed upon a sufficiently defined target. Consequently the preparation of preliminary town plans, and the surveys necessary to adapt the governing ideas to the site conditions, could proceed side by side. Much other preparatory work had also to be done before actual development started. For convenience, I give here a list of the more important matters studied or negotiated in the case of Welwyn; nearly all of which were necessary for Letchworth also.

Land Purchase: Terms of conveyances: including vendors' reservations, pre-emption rights (in case of failure of scheme), safeguards for certain tenancies, and severance of farms; fencing of new boundaries; tithe redemption, etc.

Finance: Basic estimates, on provisional periodic schedule.

Flotation of Company: Capitalization; directorate; solicitors and brokers; prospectus; advertising the issue.

Agricultural Interests: Revision of farm tenancies to permit of taking possession by stages; right of access for survey, trial holes, etc.; compensation for disturbance and tenant right. Study of soils suited to smallholdings, market gardening, etc.

Contour and Physical Survey: Levels; trees, hedges, watercourses, and features deserving preservation.

Geological Survey: Soils for different types of utilization; water sources, brick-earth, sand, chalk.

Water Supply: Technical and financial data.

Drainage and Sewage Disposal: Lines of drainage, and choice of practicable sites for outfall works.

Gas and Electricity Supply: Technical investigations as to methods and costs; decision as to whether to create new works or take supplies from existing undertakers.

Railway Facilities: Technical study as to siting of station, goods yards, factory sidings, etc.; negotiations with railway company; planning of light railway for development work.

Highways: Study of existing roads, bridle paths, footpaths; methods and costs of new construction; negotiations with Ministry of Transport, County Council, Rural District Councils.

Housing: Study of types, design and costs; negotiations with Ministry, local authorities, public utility societies, architects, contractors.

Building Regulations: Study of existing local byelaws; drafting of Company's own regulations under leases.

Land Disposal: Decisions as to principles and terms of leases, preparation of drafts, settlement of restrictive covenants; policy in fixing rentals.

Building Materials: Technical and cost investigations as to production on estate of bricks, gravel, sand, etc.

Construction: Decisions as to the agencies for development and building; respective spheres of 'direct labour' and contract work; negotiations with prospective contractors; finance and methods of reward.

Initial Buildings: Plans for temporary accommodation for development force, including housing, workshops, meals, recreation, etc.

Staff and Workers: Engagement of technicians and key personnel; inquiries as to sources of labour for development; administrative set up; provision of offices.

Forestry and Planting: Reports on woodlands and scattered trees; consideration of nursery garden for production of trees, shrubs, etc.

Town Plan: Decisions as to ultimate population; areas needed for factories, public buildings, shops, houses, open spaces; standards of density; control of design; amenities. Appointment of planning team; conferences with consultants.

Now all these matters are interrelated, and some progress had to be made with each before a preliminary town plan could be intelligently drafted, though certain elements of the plan crystallized fairly early. Many technicians had to be brought in, the basic intentions of the scheme explained to them, and their work closely co-ordinated, under the leadership of the directors and the senior administrators whom they appointed. To make the picture clearer, I describe the procedure adopted in the preparatory work at Welwyn, with which I am more familiar, referring only to Letchworth when the procedure was noticeably different.

For the physical survey some useful data was already to hand in the 6-inch and 25-inch Ordnance Survey maps; but these had to be supplemented. A firm of surveyors were asked to supervise a complete contour survey at 5 feet levels, the staff being appointed by the company. These men were the first workers on the estate, and they were boarded in farmworkers' cottages. Besides contours, they mapped the trees on the site (with species and size), hedges, field tracks, chalk pits, water courses, swallow holes, and all other physical features of possible interest.

A 6-inch geological survey map was obtainable, but proved insufficiently detailed. An eminent geologist was therefore asked to conduct exploration by trial holes all over the estate. Samples of brick-earth, sand and clay were sent to experts for making experimental bricks, tiles and paving materials, and these were duly tested. The geologist, without resorting to divining rods, was able to indicate likely sources of underground water; and trial wells were driven by a specialist firm. Water from these and from existing cottage wells was sent to analysts for tests of purity and hardness.

Engineering Considerations

Questions of water supply and drainage were gone into by a consulting engineer, who took spot-levels and reported on the practicable alternatives and most convenient layouts of the networks of mains and drains, the best positions for reservoirs and sewage disposal works, the cheapest means of providing temporary services during building, and the best order of development.

To deal with the problems of gas and electricity two consultants were appointed. They had to study not only the possibility of the company setting up its own plants, but the alternative of arranging for supplies by neighbouring statutory undertakings. As freeholder, the company could probably have provided supplies to its lessees even if the estate were within the supply area of a statutory company. But, after due examination, the Welwyn company decided to take electricity in bulk from the Northmet company and to form its own subsidiary company for distribution. Gas, on the other hand, was dealt with by an arrangement with two statutory companies whose areas met on the estate, and who amalgamated for the purpose. Letchworth followed a different route in this matter, establishing its own gasworks and power station—the latter of which now supplies an area much greater than the garden city estate.*

On railway matters another firm of consulting engineers advised the Welwyn company. They had to work out the best siting of the station and goods yard and of sidings for the first stages of development, and the layout of the sidings network for the factory area; all these schemes being of course studied in consultation with the railway company. One interesting point that at once arose was that of the land required by the railway company for its own future development. At Letchworth the railway company had not foreseen the growth of the new town, and had had to pay progressively higher prices for the land for piecemeal extensions of goods yards. At Welwyn, therefore, they bargained for the sale to them of fifty-five acres of land adjoining their line (enough for all future needs) before they would agree to any work at all. As this large area lies on both sides of the six-track railway running through the centre of the town, it is a formidable factor in the plan; a 'perimeter barrier' (to use Sir Patrick Abercrombie's term) pointing to the organization of the town into neighbourhoods east and west of the line.[1]

A full time civil engineer was appointed by each company to

[1] This is discussed on p. 94.

handle road construction and widenings, bridges, and footpaths, and to act as resident engineer for the other civil engineering works already referred to. Negotiations with the highway authorities were largely conducted by the resident engineer. The main road framework was not in either case laid out on the old grid-iron system; it was adapted to the topography after careful study. The town centre in each case almost suggested itself by the lie of the land and the appropriate siting of the railway station. In principle both road schemes are much modified spider-web systems; the main roads from the centre radiating, but with sympathy for the contours, to convenient points of confluence with the existing network in the neighbourhood. The few possible positions of crossings of the railways were a further determining factor, especially at Welwyn with its two branch lines from the central junction. Another was the stringency of the technical conditions governing the layout of the factory area. In the details of layout of access roads contours had an even more marked influence, in order to provide drainage flow, easy gradients for traffic, and pleasant sites for houses. Cul-de-sacs, small closes, squares, and the 'village green' type of layout were much used, for the sake of economy and variety of architectural grouping. Lately, perhaps, there has been some tendency to use more through roads and to reduce the proportion of closes; but I think the earlier and middle development remains the more pleasing.

Roads are costly, and as I have said, both companies had to study the utmost economy. Their experiments in the use of the narrowest possible carriageways and footpaths and the cheapest forms of construction and kerbing, and even in dispensing with paths and kerbs in some roads, are worth a word. Hard experience proved that, to provide for waiting cars and tradesmen's vans, a through residential carriageway (even at 6 to 10 houses per acre) cannot conveniently be less than 18 feet wide. A cul-de-sac carriageway must be at least 13 feet wide with a 40 feet turning point at its head. At any density above 6 houses per acre, footpaths are necessary on both sides of a through road, and on one side of a cul-de-sac of more than half a dozen houses.

The actual constructional work in both towns was undertaken by a variety of agencies. In the main such work as that of making roads, laying sewers and water-mains, and constructing sewage out-fall works, was done by direct labour under the direction of the resident engineers, to schemes prepared by them or by consulting engineers; but at Letchworth, at certain times, some of this type of constructional work was let out to contract, and practically all the building work for the company was done under contract by building firms. At Welwyn, where the company owns many factories, shops, flats and houses, and at first also owned the water and sewage disposal works, much the greater part of the constructional work for the company's own properties was undertaken by the company's own building organization under the supervision of its consulting and resident engineers and architects. The Welwyn company also, through its subsidiary building company, built a considerable number of houses for sale; whereas at Letchworth all speculative building of shops and houses was done by private building firms. In both towns many factories and houses were built for the occupiers (either to the design of the companies' architects or other architects retained by the owners themselves) under ordinary building contracts, and this method was invariably followed in the case of the Council housing schemes. I do not think the closest study of the relative experience would disclose any outstanding advantage of either the direct-labour or the contract method in the matter of cost and quality taken together. The contract method has for the estate company the advantage of elasticity if the rate of progress of the town fluctuates, since the contractors and their workers are taking up the slack. The direct-labour method both depends upon and is reciprocally an incentive towards continuity of employment; but it obviously adds to the difficulties of an estate company at times when economic circumstances hold up development. It is needless to add that capable management is indispensable to successful direct-labour work, and that the necessary senior executive personnel cannot be taken on and dispensed with at short notice.

Landscape Gardening and Tree Planting

Grass verges along roads were, after some experience, most carefully sited, prepared, and maintained. The best position is found to be between the footpath and the carriageway. If you place a grass verge between the footpath and the houses you cannot prevent its becoming (at least at any density above eight houses per acre) a bare waste of trodden earth. Newcomers from grassless cities, though they gasp with joy at the sight of green strips in roads, have to be educated not to destroy them by their pleasure in walking on them. Grass verges *can* however be preserved if properly made, properly fed and cut, and repaired immediately whenever they are damaged; but this initially expensive process must be coupled with a mobilization of public opinion on the side of grass against boots. And the battle is lost unless there are good paths of sufficient width to walk upon. Ladies in particular, with their thin, narrow shoes, will not walk on gritty gravel if there is soft grass alongside; nor will many children. After trying successively gravel, asphalt, and continuous concrete, Welwyn found that good flagged paths, well laid, are most economical, taking initial cost and maintenance together. The evidence from both towns is that very cheap construction of roads, paths and kerbs is in the long run the reverse of an economy.

Trees and planting received much attention. Welwyn engaged a landscape expert to advise on the woods and plantations already on the estate and their destiny in the plan, and on the species of trees likely to succeed on the varied soils in the town area. A nursery garden to prepare trees, shrubs and plants for use in development was one of the first things established. In both towns, also, great care was taken in the layout to avoid the loss of fine timber trees, and vast numbers of new trees, in infinite variety, were planted. The conditions governing the choice of suitable trees for street planting are severe; their lower branches must be high enough to clear the tops of umbrellas, yet their upper branches must not short-circuit the telephone wires; they may have to withstand the destructive efforts of dogs, insects, wild rabbits, and wilder human beings who cannot bear to see even sour fruits going to waste. Yet here again, assiduous maintenance and public education will enable many lovely types of trees, not commonly used, to survive.

Engineers, preoccupied with matters of great moment, can be a menace to trees. I noticed both at Letchworth and Welwyn that some fine old timber trees did not survive development. Particularly ash trees. They were unintentionally doomed by the cutting back of their roots in trenching for mains and drains. It is futile to keep a tree unless sufficient room is left for its root-spread. Elms are sometimes infected by a beetle which causes them to drop a limb without notice, making them dangerous near houses; but the beetle does not as a rule prevail unless the root-drainage of the elms is upset by the engineering. Oaks are sturdy pockets of resistance against almost any attack. It is too much to say that, by care and propaganda, street trees can be saved from all their enemies except the engineers; but the thought crosses my mind as I see in my own road a whitebeam, an exquisite foliage tree whose beauty depends much on its shape, mutilated to avoid a telephone wire. Where the same treatment is meted out to a red hawthorn ('absolutely the reddest of all red things', Pater called it) I merely sigh, for the hawthorn often finds a new shape of equal grace, but beside the distorted whitebeam I weep.

On the planting, or landscaping, of streets and precincts much may be learned by a study of the two towns. Trees were often ranged in avenue form, or in groups at intervals, in the grass verge between footways and roads. This on the face of it seems sensible, because it does help to protect the verges from pedestrians. But many trees so placed had to be too severely pruned or to vanish altogether as traffic grew and buses and lorries became more gargantuan. There followed a tendency to put the trees in one line on the front boundary of the house plots; but this can become monotonous. In my opinion more use could have been made of the actual front gardens of the houses, in addition to the fence lines and occasionally the grass verges, as sites for trees; preferably flowering or foliage trees which do not grow large or dense. Vastly greater scope is thus given. More kinds of trees can be used, and an infinite variety of effects, related to the architecture, becomes possible. In particular this treatment of front gardens as part of the whole landscaping of the street can be applied to Council and other housing schemes. There are cases at Letchworth and Welwyn where this has been done with outstanding success. The cost is negligible; a few shillings per house will work wonders.

Expert knowledge and taste proved necessary both for good planting and for maintenance. It is not a matter that should be left to the architect, or the council surveyor, though both must have a say in it. Towns should have their landscape architects and foresters, or persons of equal skill, at least as consultants.*

Agricultural Considerations

One of the first things necessary, before work could proceed on the sites, was to come to terms with the farmers, who were of course in occupation of all the land and almost all the buildings. In general they could hardly be expected to hail with joy the prospect that a town of 35,000 or 40,000 was being planned on their holdings. I don't know how it was at Letchworth, but at Welwyn the apprehension of the farmers was qualified by a deep-rooted conviction that the whole thing was lunacy and would come to nothing. Farmers, however, are not given to indecent rigidity in business affairs. G. K. Chesterton said of the Irish during the troubles of 1916, 'Under the patriot who fights there is always the peasant who bargains.' It was found possible to negotiate access for survey, and possession of land needed for the first building and road sites, on reasonable terms. Expert agricultural surveyors were engaged to settle these terms, which involve mysteries of tenant right, dilapidations, and other matters dark to the urban layman.

Holdings had to be to some extent rearranged, and tenancy agreements revised, so that, in the areas designated for building, land could be taken over as and when required. Land likely to be wanted soon was taken out of regular crop rotation, but arrangements were made with the farmers to keep it in order and free of weeds. Certain land was selected for use as small holdings; but this was a minor element at Letchworth and Welwyn, where in general the land was not suitable for market gardening, though a few fruit farms and nursery gardens have been successfully established. At Letchworth, where the agricultural estate was extensive, one of the full time officers of the company was a man with rural land-agency experience. At Welwyn, rather surprisingly, one of the dispossessed farmers (Mr. W. C. Horn) took a most enthusiastic interest in the whole project, and besides throwing himself energetically into public work and becoming a member, and for a time chairman, of the local authority, acted as agricultural adviser to the company in dealing with its remaining farm tenancies.

Though it came later, it is convenient to mention here that at Welwyn an experiment was made, in the hey-day of the National Guilds movement, in farming the whole of the agricultural land

of the estate by a body called the New Town Agricultural Guild—
which raised its own finance independently of the Welwyn company, and worked on the limited dividend principle, the farmworkers being represented on its management committee. Not
being myself knowledgeable about what James Joyce called
'Angricultural and Prepostoral Ouraganizations', I am not able
to evaluate this experiment. It did not succeed financially, and
it was wound up after a few years, leaving however some interesting and not valueless marks on the structure of the town. The
land was relet, in rather small farms, to a number of independent
holders. At Letchworth, independent farmers have cultivated the
agricultural belt throughout.*

Evolution of the Town Plan

The procedure in working out the plans of the two garden cities
differed considerably. When Letchworth was started the directors
had no precedent to go on, and though their broad intention was
governed by Ebenezer Howard's well-thought-out diagram,
adaptation to an actual site presented a whole series of novel
problems. As soon as the contour survey had been completed, two
firms of architects were invited to submit layout plans for the
company's consideration. The choice fell on the plan prepared by
Raymond Unwin and Barry Parker, then almost unknown. They
proved a partnership of imagination, decision and taste; and it was
they who did in fact settle the main features of the plan. By common consent this Letchworth plan was a notable advance in town
layout—all the more remarkable because the architect-planners
had not had previous experience of development on a large scale.*
At Welwyn the plan was the work of a much larger team. A
consulting architect-planner prepared the preliminary general
sketch. He was given a good deal of data: the maximum population to be allowed for, and the areas estimated to be needed for
the zones for industry, shops and public buildings, houses, and
open spaces. He received the contour maps and reports of other
experts as they were produced, and there was close and prolonged
deliberation on all aspects of the plan between all the experts, a
committee of the directors, and the principal officers of the company.
Thus there was no single all-knowing town planner. The architect-

planner expressed in drawings, first as sketches, and gradually with more definition and detail, the results of the work of a team of which he was a member.

I well remember one of the conferences on the plan of Welwyn. It took place when the surveys were far enough on for the possibilities and limiting factors of the site to be grasped by all concerned, and the intentions of the promoting group had been made clear to the experts. At this meeting, under the chairmanship of Capt. R. L. Reiss, the basic principles to be followed in planning were defined. Each expert then stated his provisional conclusions in his own field, giving some idea of the possible order of development, and rough estimates of the cost of initial instalments, sometimes on alternative policies. I doubt if any such assembly had taken place in England since the days of Edward I, when he was thinking about building Berwick-on-Tweed; nor do I think, judging by the results, that King Edward could have had so adequate a team.[1]

Thereafter the main elements of the plan rapidly crystallized. But innumerable exchanges of view and exhaustive discussions went on. The nucleus who sat through all the discussions consisted of the three directors who took the main responsibility, the estate manager of the company, the resident engineer, and the architect-planner. The drawings were produced by the two last-named, who were of course in constant touch with each other on technical details.

To sum up the planning procedure. The Letchworth plan, subject to observance of the principles derived from Howard's book, was produced by two technicians—one of whom (Raymond Unwin) happened to be a man of exceptional breadth of outlook. The judgment of the Letchworth directors was nowhere better shown than in their choice for this work of one of the few men who

---

[1] But it is interesting to note that of the fifty or so persons called together for Edward I's conference in 1296 on the Berwick plan, four were specialists in town planning, and at least one had had experience in laying out the earlier new town of Winchelsea (1280). In turn the Winchelsea plan had had the benefit of the experience of a Gascon planner familiar with the development of the Bastide towns in France. Thus King Edward clearly recognized the value in town-building both of team work and of the passing on of the 'know-how' gained in practical experience. See *Calendar of Patent Rolls*, 1280–83; and T. F. Tout, *Medieval Town Planning* (1917).

subsequently proved able to integrate the social and technical factors in the new art of town-development. No one was then available with experience of planning a town *de novo*—though the valuable experience of Bournville, Port Sunlight and the Trafford Park Industrial Estate were in fact drawn upon by some of the persons engaged on the scheme.

The Welwyn plan was produced by an organized team, containing many able specialists, and led by directors whose experience of the Letchworth precedents showed them what to follow and what to avoid. Their architect-planner (Louis de Soissons, A.R.A.) was a technician with a rapid grasp of a physical problem, the power of clear thinking, and sure taste; he accepted the aims and the social and economic data from the promoting group. The working out of the Welwyn plan was pushed forward with great boldness, competence and speed. I am sure the foundations could not have been so well laid without the personal participation of men who had been through the parallel phases at Letchworth and had subsequently reflected critically on that experience. Again and again time was saved and mistakes avoided through this knowledge.*

Chapter IV

THE LAND: ITS USE AND CONTROL

Planning through Lease Covenants

Fundamental to Howard's scheme was that the garden city companies should retain the ownership of the freehold (with exceptions only for certain public buildings) and should yield possession only subject to covenants limiting the future use of the land. At the same time it was considered axiomatic to leave the maximum freedom to firms and individuals within these limits. Much thought was given to the best way to ensure the necessary planning control, while retaining for the companies (as trustees for the community) as much as practicable of future increments of value. In both towns the 'building lease' was adopted as the method. Standard lease forms were prepared, which were varied in detail to meet particular cases, but some clauses of which were insisted upon. The forms were evolved as a result of experience, and the latest versions are worth study by anyone responsible for large-scale development or redevelopment.

Letchworth granted, for most types of property, leases for 99 years at a fixed ground rent, or for 198 years ('two 99's') or 999 years ('three nines') revisible every 99 years. For factories, only leases for 999 years at a fixed rent were granted. Welwyn, for all but shops, granted leases of 999 years at a fixed rent; and at first for shop properties leases of 99 years. (Later it ceased to grant any building leases for shops, for reasons I explain in my section on Retail Trading.)

Such long leases, of course, inevitably passed over to the lessee the benefit of increases of value within the term—no negligible factor in a rapidly growing town. Both companies were well aware of this. But they had to be practical. The public were not compelled to come to the garden cities, and had to be conciliated. Welwyn standardized the 999 years' lease for all but shops, in the belief that the value of house and factory sites (tied down to those uses by covenants) was not likely to multiply to such an extent as to matter. Most individual lessees accepted a 999 years' lease as virtually a freehold; the end of a 99 years' period seemed to some to loom too nearly ahead. And anyway the directors thought the difference hardly worth arguing about, feeling that the land system of this country would probably alter very much within a century.

In the case of factory sites, industrialists building factories were found to be dynastic by instinct; they hated mere 99 years' leases; and both companies were most anxious to attract industries and not disposed to stand on a point that seemed academic. Theoretically, the garden city companies would have preferred ground rents revisible by periodic revaluations (a method tried, with no very shining success, in some American communities). But lessees were disinclined to invest money in buildings with uncertainty as to their future outgoings for ground rent. In fact there were some applicants for sites who so strongly objected to anything but freehold property that they would not accept even a 999 years' lease. These, to the companies' regret and their own loss, stayed away from the garden cities. If in the ordinary towns of their choice they subsequently found fried-fish shops built next door to their desirable villa residences, perhaps it was poetic justice. The prejudice against the leasehold system diminished as people came to realize the advantages of planning control.*

Though care was taken not to make the leases onerous, the few covenants necessary to safeguard the planning principles were made very definite. Every lease limits the use of the land to some one specific purpose. A site leased for the building of a dwelling house may not be used for any kind of manufacture or trade or the sale of goods. A site leased for a factory can only be used for manufacturing industry (usually, at Welwyn, for a specified type of industry), and not for a shop or dwellings—except, in the case of large sites, one dwelling for a resident caretaker. Leases of shop sites all exclude manufacture. The shop leases at Letchworth permitted retail trade of any class; but the Welwyn leases laid down limits for the kind of retail trade. (Later, as I explain in my section on Retail Trade, Welwyn discontinued granting any building leases at all to retailers or shop-property builders.)

All leases in both towns preclude the sale of intoxicating liquor on all premises except those leased for the purpose. Thus even a 'club licence' cannot be obtained except with the consent of the estate companies. At Letchworth no new lease has been granted for any public house or licensed premises. There is an interesting history behind this. When the town was founded there was a strong national movement for prohibition of the manufacture and sale of drink: a movement parallel to that which in the United States led to total prohibition by an amendment to the Federal Constitution. There was also a less drastic movement for 'local option', under which it was proposed that any town or district could prohibit licensed premises in its area by a referendum of the electors; this system was actually adopted for Scotland. The directors of Letchworth decided to apply 'local option' in the new town; and the matter has been voted upon by adult suffrage several times—always with a substantial majority against any new licence, though there are three pre-garden city public houses in villages on the outskirts of the estate. One club registration (that of the Conservative Club) slipped through by a mistake in a lease. Otherwise the central area of Letchworth to this day remains 'dry' by the will of the inhabitants.*

At Welwyn the directors did not adopt local option. Their policy has been to lease sites for a moderate number of licensed premises, on condition that they are conducted on the principles in force in the state-owned public houses of the Carlisle district— that meals must be provided as well as drinks, and that the managers are allowed no commission on drink sales. Recently, also, it has become the policy to give permission for 'club licences' for factory clubs and canteens and the larger social clubs, subject to certain not onerous rules.

What this all amounts to, of course, is that, in the two garden cities, the practice of 'use zoning' now coming into general favour under statutory planning was from the first secured by covenants under leases.

The leases also prescribe observance of building lines and building areas, and require compliance with the building regulations of the estates, as well as with the byelaws of the local authority so far as they apply. Thus housing schemes, though exempted from the byelaws, are subject to the companies' building regulations. It is interesting that, in these two towns, the local authorities, as well as the public utility housing societies, are lessees of the estate companies and technically subject to the same covenants as other house owners.

The plans and external appearance and materials of all buildings, including extensions, are subject under the leases to the approval of the companies' architects. Advertisements on buildings are not allowed without express consent—except for one name-sign on each business building, of a type to be approved in detail. This gives complete architectural control. (The operation of this control, which raises interesting problems, is referred to later.) Guidance is given in the building regulations as to the standards used in approving designs, which cover such matters as the orientation of rooms for sun, the placing of outbuildings, the design of backs as well as fronts of buildings, and the character of fences and hedges. The conservation of top soil in the course of construction was required in both towns from the start. And there are covenants requiring the preservation of timber trees (which may not be lopped without consent), the care of hedges and cultivation of gardens, and in some cases the retention of a layout of open forecourts and the prohibition of fences or hedges which would spoil such a layout. (At Welwyn this last precaution was omitted in the earlier leases, and one or two individualist lessees enclosed their front gardens—which had been carefully landscaped with the street as a whole on an open treatment—to the extreme annoyance of other lessees who were attracted to the street by the open treatment.)*

Both towns had special lease covenants requiring lessees to contribute to the cost of repairing and lighting the estate roads so long as they remained private roads; besides the more usual clauses requiring lessees to pay making-up charges levied by the local authority when taking over roads. Letchworth actually enforced these charges, and they proved a source of some dispute and irritation. Welwyn never in fact enforced them; a special arrangement was made with the local authority, under a little used provision of the Private Street Works Act, for the early taking over of roads without charge on the frontagers—the cost of surfacing and kerbing being charged on the rates. This was equitable in a new town, where virtually all properties were newly built. It would not be equitable where the rate-charge would extend over old properties whose owners had paid direct making-up charges in the past. It proved a good method, avoiding much friction and speeding up the finishing-off and taking over of roads.

Industrial Development

Careful study was given to the layout and development of the factory zones. The area likely to be needed was calculated on the experience of existing specialized industrial areas—those at Trafford Park and in Chicago, for example. In calculating the requirements at Welwyn it was originally estimated that about fifty persons would be employed per industrial acre. This was not a bad shot, but space requirements for factories (as for most other town purposes) are rising; and the larger factories demand more land for future expansion than was anticipated. Both Letchworth and Welwyn have found it necessary to increase their allocation for industrial purposes.

The greater part of the factory accommodation at Letchworth, and a good deal of that at Welwyn, was built by manufacturers themselves on 999-year building leases. But the tendency has been more and more towards the provision of factory space on rental. Letchworth began this with a three-storey sectional factory let out in floors; but found that one-storey sectional factories were of much greater practical utility and therefore more in demand. Welwyn went in extensively for one-storey sectional factories, many of them with two-storey office blocks on the road frontage; and this proved a most successful way of attracting small and medium-sized firms, some of which grew to large undertakings.

The sectional factories were of an economical type of construction, costing in pre-war days from eight to ten shillings per square foot. They were let on repairing leases of from one to twenty-one years, and so arranged that firms could have small units to start with and take more space as and when they needed it. In both towns these factories proved in themselves a remunerative investment, and at Welwyn they played a large part in attracting new industries. The simple types of buildings evolved deserve study in comparison with those of trading estates elsewhere; they were on the whole better and more pleasing in appearance than those of some commercial estates, while considerably less costly than those on some of the government trading estates.

Extension space, and ample yard space for unloading and loading, storage of packing materials and sometimes of wastes, and forethought for the siting of additional lavatories, outbuildings and cycle-sheds, proved very important. The appetite for parking-space for cars and cycles continually grows and must be foreseen. Untidiness of the back yards of factories cannot be altogether avoided. A good deal of six-foot fencing or walling is therefore called for. It was found necessary, also, that great care should be taken to isolate factory yards and back roads from the nearest dwelling houses and their gardens by tree belts 40 to 50 feet wide and thickly enough planted to produce invisibility.

Noise has been found to be a factor making reasonable isolation from dwellings very desirable. Another factor pointing the same way is the inevitable coming and going of numbers of workers, usually in a hurry, and using many cars and bicycles. The suggestion of some planning writers that factories and workshops can be dotted about among dwellings must be frowned on in the light of garden city experience. This does not imply, however, except in the case of heavy industry, that factories need to be at any great distance from housing areas. But they must be far enough away for the noise of machinery not to be heard. And in planning it must be borne in mind that a factory originally built for a nice clean industry, employing a few tidily-dressed people, may later come to be occupied by an industry employing larger numbers, on relatively dirty processes, and perhaps with machinery running day and night. On the other hand, it is not very likely that a light factory will ever be converted into a blast furnace or rolling mill. A reasonable degree of isolation, coupled with discretion in reletting, will protect the amenities of the neighbouring residents beyond the tree belt. It is practicable administratively to avoid letting the factories nearest the houses for smelly or smoky processes. It is not so easy to prevent the growth of the numbers employed, or the increasing use of machinery which may make a continuous if not very loud noise by day or night.

Upkeep of the external appearance and decoration of factories, and proper care of grass and trees on the public side of them, are most important, and have been found to require constant watchfulness and tactful insistence. But as these things are in the interest of the industrial firms as well of the estate, they are not a serious problem for competent administrators.

The great variety of industries in the garden cities goes to show the immense scope there is for decentralization to towns of this character. No particular type predominates. Of course the extractive industries, and others perforce located close to sources of raw materials, are absent. But the industries are not all 'light' as the term is commonly used. 'Medium heavy' industry is present: for example the fabrication of constructional steel work, iron founding, and steel casting. This reveals the important locational fact that heavy materials can be put through manufacturing processes on sites intermediate between the points of basic production and the places of utilization or shipment.

The materials used for garden city manufactures are mostly either valuable in ratio to bulk or weight, or, where they are not so, enter into products which are valuable in ratio to bulk or weight. Whether raw or semi-fabricated, they come from all over the world, and some of the goods manufactured go out all over the world, and most of them all over Great Britain or a large area thereof. This wide range of sources and destinations is of course a growing characteristic of modern industry. It tends to free industry from a narrow compulsion in location. In theory, for transport economy, processes should occur somewhere on the straight line of route between the winning of raw materials from the earth and the delivery of finished goods to the consumer. But as both the sources and the consumers are spread country-wide or world-wide, a great number of potential manufacturing points exist on the criss-crossing lines of route between them. This and the cheapness and speed of modern transport account for the increasing elasticity of location of so much modern industry.

Manufacturers thus having a choice of sites in regard to the movement of goods are able to give more weight to such other factors as convenience of premises, operating conditions, light and space, and the health and the social and home surroundings of their personnel. Some firms coming to the garden cities frankly put living conditions in the forefront, as a matter of human decency. But many firms (it is a convention in some business circles) repudiate such motives as unbusiness-like sentiment. Actually there is no conflict. Living conditions are now, for many industries, economically more important than marginal variations of the cost of transport on materials and products as between a number of alternative situations. With the rising status of workers in industry as self-respecting partners, rather than as disposable 'hands', these once imponderable factors become of real weight, altogether apart from sentiment.

The varied industries already in the garden cities by no means exhaust the types that could be so located. There are however limiting factors worth mentioning. One is scale. Obviously a very large factory will have difficulties in an area with a disproportionately small working population. When just before the war Letchworth and Welwyn were towns of between 15,000 and 18,000 (with some further population within employable range) their largest factories employed from 1,000 to 1,500 workers, which was felt to be at or near the convenient upward limit. Size matters much less if the firm's pay-roll is constant. It is fluctuation, whether seasonal or cyclical, that creates difficulties both for towns and firms.

It is not socially a bad thing that in a moderate-sized town the fluctuations of a firm's employment come more conspicuously to notice. In a great city the evils of seasonal unemployment, and of the decline and failure of firms, are not always immediately corrected by the picking up of new jobs by displaced workers; they are often merely hidden in the mass. Industrialists can, by their own planning, do something to reduce seasonal fluctuations, and in a small town they have strong incentives to do so. The network of employment exchanges has largely replaced the queue at the factory gate as a means of adjusting shifts of employment on the rise and fall of firms. A full employment policy (as was evident in wartime) forces on firms the utmost forethought for continuity. All these trends are reducing the dependence of industry on the rather inhuman convenience of an elastic labour 'pool'. Life is being made harder for production planners thereby, but less hard for operatives. All the same, very large establishments in small towns tend to run into difficulties. And a reasonable diversity of industries is helpful in the taking up of slack when particular firms have to dismiss personnel.

Many industrialists are now disposed to think that, for organizational reasons, it is desirable to limit the size of production units. No agreement has been reached as to the optimum size in most industries, and it is likely to vary between industries. One big engineering firm, employing over 20,000 in all, has in recent years worked on the principle that the optimum for a single factory is about 500 workers, and has dispersed units of that size over a whole region, maintaining central design, purchase, and production planning. A general theory has not yet crystallized. When the 'community' factors of the equation are brought in, with their bearing on journeys to work and workers' enthusiasm for their jobs, these are likely to influence greatly the overall calculation. The still prevailing idea that industrial establishments must inevitably continue to increase in scale is based on mechanical thinking.*

A second limiting factor is industrial 'linkage'. Though the crisscross of supply and dispatch indicates an infinite number of possible points of manufacture, many factories depend on the products of other types of factories already predominantly located in certain districts. Suppliers and supplied cannot be too far apart, not only for reasons of speed and economy in the transit of goods, but also because there has to be frequent inter-visiting between technicians and commercial personnel, and this is important in changing and competitive industries. The limitation can be exaggerated. In many cases it is no great inconvenience for firms with this relationship to be twenty-five to fifty miles apart—a car drive of an hour or so for persons or urgently needed bits and pieces. But it is seriously uneconomic for closely linked firms to be in widely distant regions.

Letchworth and Welwyn have many industries thus linked with other firms in the London region. Their experience proves that decentralization of linked industries to towns at distances of twenty-five or thirty-five miles creates no serious difficulty; the disadvantages of this degree of separation are outweighed by the advantages of a better or more economical situation for manufacture. Either suppliers or supplied can be in satellite towns within this range at least, and probably within somewhat wider range. It would be easier still if the road communications within London itself were decongested by the process of dispersal. Half the time required for the twenty-two-mile journey from Welwyn to the centre of London is taken by the last five or six miles.

This latitude in the siting even of linked industries is often overlooked in discussions of the policy of dispersal from such integrated
manufacturing centres as London or Birmingham. It is extreme
to argue that their industries can be compelled or induced to move
to different regions altogether, or that new firms of the same
classes should not be allowed to settle in the region of their natural
linkages, which would mean that many could not come into
existence at all. On the other hand far too heavy weather is made
of linkages as an argument even against restriction of settlement
in congested centres and medium-distance dispersal from such
centres. Both arguments lack common sense. A very large proportion of these linked city industries could be carried on in
satellite towns. The difficulties of transfer (which I discuss in
Chapter VIII) are the temporary ones inherent in any uprooting
and replanting—not in the operation of the factories after removal. Linkages can be stretched. But they cannot safely be broken.

The experience of Letchworth and Welwyn shows that site-
association, or grouping of a number of industries in a planned
and properly equipped industrial zone, is advantageous. This is
not the same thing as 'linkage'. Some confusion has been caused
by the assumption that the alternative to concentration in very
large cities is the dotting of single industries in rural areas. Professor Sargant Florence, who has done much original work on the
theory of industrial location, uses the word 'dispersion' in this
sense; and proves, well enough, that there are few city industries
adapted to it.[1] It is important to be clear that rural 'dispersion'
in this sense (the word for which should really be 'diffusion')[2] has
nothing to do with 'dispersal' as the term is consistently used in
this book. It is in general most undesirable that factories of the
urban type, or likely to grow to substantial size, should be placed
in isolated rural villages, unless these villages are intended to be
developed into country towns of at least 15,000 population.

In the two garden cities the scale of factory businesses varies as
widely as their types. Besides a very few of over 1,000, there are
many employing 100 to 500 workers, many from 25 to 100, and
many even smaller. Sectional factories on rental have proved a

[1] See P. Sargant Florence: 'The Selection of Industries suitable for Dispersion
into Rural Areas', in *Journal of the Royal Statistical Society*, Part II, 1944.
[2] See Chapter VII.

useful means of giving a start to new firms; one firm in Welwyn began with three people in a factory of 1,500 square feet, and expanded in ten years to 1,000 people (and to over 2,000 during the war years). Some firms beginning in rented premises later built factories for themselves. The majority at Letchworth, and many at Welwyn, took sites and provided their own buildings from the start. The survival rate has been high. As everywhere, some firms fail; but very few have left either town for other places.

Perhaps the engineering and metal-working group is the largest. It includes the manufacture of motor-cars, lorries, lawn mowers, motor-cycle components, printing and paper-folding machinery, mining and other machinery, tools and jigs, compressors, aeroplane parts, gas water heaters, lead pipe and sheeting, iron, steel and non-ferrous castings, coppered steel tubing, chains, baby carriages, tabulating machines and other office appliances, steel furniture, locks and fittings, pressed parts, carpenters' tools, and constructional steelwork. The electrical group includes radio and television sets, electronics, electrical components, welding apparatus, heating installations, heaters, and lighting fittings. There are firms making grinding wheels and refractory tiles, bricks, abrasive papers, lenses, and many types of scientific instruments. Printing and bookbinding and furniture making and woodwork are fairly important. Industries dealing with textiles include the manufacture of parachutes, corsets, racquet-strings, embroidery, and silk dresses. The food group ranges from shredded wheat, macaroni, margarine, nursery biscuits and food extracts, to sugar confectionery. The chemical group covers fine drugs, the synthesis of vitamins, plastics, toothpaste, cosmetics, adhesive plasters, and industrial chemicals. There are a number of research laboratories, apart from those attached to particular factories. And miscellaneous industries include film studios, seed growing, nursery gardening, fruit growing, poultry raising, and the manufacture of photographic paper, rubber goods, advertising tape, oiled silk, and matches. In addition to these industries, which make for a wide market, there are, as in any town, the ancillary and repair industries which cater for the factory zone and the rest of the community.

During the second World War, a large number (probably the majority) of factories in Letchworth and Welwyn have turned over to war work. Many transferred workers have been added to the population, and there has been intense pressure on the towns. They have made, in research and development as well as in quantity of production, no small contribution to the war effort. Conversely, some peace-time industries have been compulsorily closed down, and their premises requisitioned for war production; among these may be some of those listed above. A feature of the war has been the evacuation to the garden cities, as to other country towns, of firms from London, and of particular interest is the temporary dispersal of non-industrial businesses of the head office type. Many of these would be capable of permanent dispersal, provided that suitable premises and adequate housing were made available.*

Retail Trade and Shopping Policy

Shopping centres present a whole series of problems, and the founders of Letchworth and Welwyn gave prolonged thought to the manner of their development. There is no point of policy on which the two towns differ more. In studying their experience it must be borne in mind that both towns excluded any sort of trading from private dwelling houses, unless with specific consent. This prevented the growth of scattered little shops, common in nearly all towns. It forced the concentration of retail trading in areas selected for that purpose; and of course, gave the estate companies power to control, to any extent they thought desirable (always within the limits that people would tolerate without refusing to settle in the towns) the number, size, and character of shops. Letchworth exercised this control to some extent; Welwyn carried it much further.

The Letchworth company granted building leases for shops, the buildings being provided by speculative builders or investors in shop property who let shops to traders, and in some cases by retail trading firms for their own occupation. Except that the depths of plots, and with more elasticity their frontages and the character of the buildings, were controlled by the plan, there was no definite policy of limitation; sites were let in the main shopping centre as applicants came along, at ground rents they were at the time able and willing to pay. The first shop sites were leased for 99 years at ground rents as low as £1 16s. 3d. to £3 2s. 6d. per plot, equivalent to £10 per acre, per annum; this of course was when the town was just beginning, and population and available turnover were small. As the town grew, new shop sites were let, still on 99-year leases, at higher ground rents. As a result a busy shopping centre has been created on a basis of free and open competition—the centre benefiting by the fact that the diffusion of part of the available trade over shops in dwelling-house areas has been precluded. Most of the original traders were individuals, but when the population grew substantial, branches of multiple-shop firms came along—in some cases building their own premises, in some cases renting premises from shop-property owners, and in other cases acquiring or displacing existing private businesses. By mid-1939, when the population had reached about 18,000, there were 172 shops in the main centre, and nine shops in a few small sub-centres. This is about one shop per 100 inhabitants, which may be compared to about one in forty to forty-five in the older towns in Hertfordshire and most other parts of the country, where dwelling-house shops had not been precluded by planning; a considerable difference, but still leaving the average shop rather small and a proportion of traders barely able to obtain sufficient turnover for survival and efficiency.

On the other hand, the earlier traders who own their shops on building leases retain the benefit of a very low ground rent; and shop-property owners who took sites on lease at the earlier ground rents are able to obtain from the retailers who are now their tenants considerably enhanced occupation rents. These are really gaining, not merely the results of their enterprise—the normal goodwill of established businesses—but also the increment of land-rental value due to the growth of the town and the expenditure of the estate company; and they will continue to do so until the 99-year leases expire. They would argue that they are entitled to this 'profit rental' or its equivalent because they took a chance on the future of Letchworth when it was highly speculative. Against this, it can be replied that in general the ground rents negotiated at any given time were not appreciably in advance of the land value appropriate to the then population.

The Welwyn company had this experience very much in mind

in shaping their policy. When Welwyn was started (in 1920) the cost of building was abnormally high and, though invitations were extended, few if any traders could be found willing to commit themselves to building on leased sites the sort of shops which the company considered appropriate to the town they intended to develop. There was a very natural difference of outlook. The company were thinking of a populous industrial town, with the full intention of making it a reality in ten or twenty years. A trader, or a shop-property investor, could see only a tiny rural population of 400 people scattered over four square miles, a few huts for workers, foundations for a score or two of houses, and a plan on paper. Therefore, even the more adventurous of them would not offer to go further than a temporary wooden shop with an option to convert it into a permanent building at an almost nominal ground rent if and when so many thousand inhabitants had arrived. From the prospective trader's point of view this was ordinary business caution. From the garden city company's point of view it was heads you win, tails we lose.

Further, even on these lines, only a few shops, and these of the safest bread-and-butter kind, picking the eyes out of potential local business and giving an incomplete service to the early residents, could possibly have been arranged for, and in unsatisfactory temporary premises at that. The company wanted an all-round shopping service in decent premises as soon as possible, covering classes of goods for which there would not for some years be enough turnover to sustain specialized shops. They therefore approached the co-operative movement to see whether they would set up a general service stores, offering them a monopoly for a period of years in order to give reasonable security for their investment. At that time the Co-operative Union was wedded to the strict traditional theory that a co-operative stores must be based on local consumer membership from the start. They pointed out that the estate was already within the area of the St. Albans Co-operative Society, which could start a branch in the new town; that Society was accordingly approached, but decided, on similar principles, that it could not do so until there were sufficient local consumers to justify it.

It is of interest that some years later (at a conference in Middlesbrough) the Co-operative Congress gave the Co-operative Wholesale Society powers to initiate new societies in areas where development could be anticipated. Very probably, if this decision had taken place before Welwyn was started, the first shop in the town would have been a co-operative stores.[1]

As things were, the Welwyn company decided that the only way to provide a good all-round shopping service in the early years was to form a subsidiary of their own, to build and manage a departmental stores. Further capital being necessary for this purpose, a monopoly for ten years was given to this subsidiary in order to enable it to offer reasonable prospects to its investors; though as it was under the control of the parent company it remained open for the subsidiary to waive its rights if rapid growth permitted the admission of additional shops before the expiry of the ten years—and some competing shops were in fact admitted within the period. In arriving at the original decision, individual directors were actuated by different reasons. Some believed that the 'rationalization' of the shopping service by starting with one large stores was in itself a better method than the gradual evolution of a shopping centre by the process followed at Letchworth; a view for which the case is obvious. This line of thought was seconded by the fact that the policy would conserve land values for the future; no long leases need be 'given away' to outside interests at low ground rents. Other directors felt that, while free (or partially restricted) competition might theoretically be better, the economic circumstances of the time and situation pointed to the monopoly subsidiary as the wisest practicable expedient for a period. All agreed that the monopoly should only last for a limited time; it was always intended to admit competing shops as soon as possible, even if the original stores business continued to be run by the company.

This is the origin of the Welwyn Stores, which has become a notable and characteristic feature of the town. From its beginning in 1921 its policy has been to supply all kinds of goods for all levels of income, which involved starting many unremunerative departments, supported by those with a more substantial turnover.

---

[1] Ebenezer Howard had made strenuous efforts to persuade the Co-operative Wholesale Society to provide a complete shopping service on bold and imaginative lines for Letchworth when that town was started in 1904, but was unsuccessful—no doubt for the same reasons.

Being the only easily accessible shop for the growing population, the stores could not pick and choose the classes of goods it would sell; it had to be run as a 'universal provider' whether or not particular lines were in sufficient demand to be remuneratively stocked, which made its management exceptionally difficult; and, further, having for years a monopoly position, it would have been a natural target for criticism, even if its management had been at all times perfect, which it was not. Housed at first in semi-temporary one-storey buildings of a novel type, the Welwyn Stores transferred in 1939 to a magnificent building which also contains offices, residential flats, clubrooms and sports facilities, and a very charming restaurant. It is a remarkable institution for a town which by 1939 had reached a population of about 15,000; most of its departments are now competently run, and in my opinion it gives a retail service superior in important respects to that which could have been provided in any other way. It is the daily rendezvous, the true market place, of the town, and at present handles something like half the town's total retail turnover.*

Competition has never been in fact absent. From the earliest days traders in the nearby small towns of Hatfield and Old Welwyn have maintained house-to-house delivery services, and there were not wanting itinerant tradesmen to cater for the desire for choice and personal service. The old-established and lively market centres of St. Albans and Hertford are within an easy bus ride; at one time most housewives made periodical shopping expeditions to these towns, whose inhabitants now increasingly return the compliment by visiting the garden city stores and shopping centre—an entirely healthy and pleasant exchange.

The policy of the Welwyn company since about 1930 has been to admit a limited number of additional retail traders so that there shall be competition in the supply of all classes of goods, while at the same time traders may have scope for enough turnover for proper stocking, efficient service, and a decent livelihood. But with two early exceptions, building leases have not been granted to traders or outside investors in commercial properties. The company, through another subsidiary, itself builds shops and lets them on occupation leases for seven, fourteen or twenty-one years at progressive rentals and for defined trades. Multiple firms (Boots, W. H. Smith, etc.), as well as the Co-operative Society, which came in when the town was well established, hold their shops on these terms. In the main shopping centre, and in the Peartree neighbourhood centre, there are now nearly forty shops, apart from the Welwyn Stores, which in addition to its great central emporium, has four carefully sited branches. The war held up the building of a further score of shops for letting.*

Without doubt the Welwyn policy of building shop premises for rental on short leases has proved sound. It makes all the difference to the financial return on the development of a growing town; it enables greater architectural harmony to be achieved; and it permits of a policy of definition of the class of goods to be dealt in by each shop, giving fair play to traders while ensuring competition.

The policy of starting with a big departmental stores having a monopoly for a period is more controversial. At Welwyn there has been much local criticism of the system, though I do not think the critics have always analysed the merits of the alternatives. It is arguable that any degree of restriction holds back the popularity of a shopping centre and deters new residents from settling in the town; and that the estate company might, by being less concerned for the future increment of value on early leases, have secured a quicker growth of population and a better total financial return. But the opposite argument seems to me stronger; that a collection of scruffy struggling shops in temporary or cheap premises would even more seriously check development. The right speed for the admission of retail businesses must in any case be a matter of judgment, and a difficult one; and I do think it probable, on balance, that Welwyn would have been wise to admit independent traders a little more rapidly. In principle the Welwyn policy seems to me correct. To start the shopping centre with an estate-controlled departmental stores, and to introduce competing traders in each class of business later is, I think, best from the point of view of service to the inhabitants and from that of the conservation of values.

But it must be faced that the inhabitants of a town will not all agree with this. The Welwyn Stores, being for years the one indispensable shop, whether customers like it or not, was (very properly) expected to behave as a public service and to sell everything asked for at the lowest price; while at the same time it was under fire as a monopoly assumed to be bent upon exploitation and tyranny. If you want something, and after running round to three or four shops you cannot get it, the shortcomings of one trader are to some extent excused by the equal shortcomings of the others; if there is only one shop that palliative does not suggest itself. On the other hand, there is convenience and pleasantness in shopping in a great and beautiful building, where you meet lots of people you know and the atmosphere is spacious and cheerful.

The Welwyn Stores has its enthusiasts, and if it were whisked away by some Genie of the Lamp, it would be sadly missed; even people who criticize it display it with pride to visiting friends. It has stamped itself indelibly into the personality of the town.

It should be added that both at Letchworth and Welwyn attention was paid to the arrangement, structure and appearance of shops with the intention to create convenient and dignified centres. One-storey buildings have rarely been permitted; as a general rule shop buildings are of two or three storeys, the upper floors being used at Letchworth either as residential premises for traders, or as commercial offices, and at Welwyn as commercial offices or self-contained flats. At Letchworth the shop buildings were designed by different architects, subject to the approval of the estate architect; at Welwyn the main shopping streets were designed as a whole by one architect—a policy made easier by the fact that almost all the buildings in the centre are owned by the company or its subsidiaries. I deal elsewhere with the architectural question.

Public Buildings, Schools and Open Spaces

In both towns the chief public buildings are grouped in the main centre. They include of course council offices, estate offices, fire stations, cinemas, public offices, hotels and refreshment houses, and some of the principal assembly halls. Letchworth has also placed its public library, museum, and county grammar school in the centre, and its fine swimming pool near by; and Welwyn has the intention of centralizing its county college (for further education), library, museum, theatre, art gallery, and chief swimming pool. Welwyn's county grammar school, on the other hand, is on the edge of the town. Churches in both towns are fairly widely distributed, as also are the smaller halls and meeting-rooms. Clubs also are dispersed, some of them in the sub-centres of neighbourhood units. Public-houses at Letchworth only exist in the outlying villages embraced by the town, for reasons I have already given: at Welwyn the new ones are in the main and subsidiary centres, and the older ones towards the outskirts.

As in other towns, but rather more systematically, public primary schools and private schools are distributed in relation to the school population. Regrouping under the proposals of the new Education Act presents, as elsewhere, considerable problems. The increasing demand for playing-field space around schools is a problem in itself. When the two towns were laid out the education authorities considered one and a half to two acres enough for a primary school for 400 children. Nowadays they want six acres (if they can get it); while for a secondary school of 400 twelve acres is considered desirable. Even a garden city finds it difficult to meet these growing demands.[1]*

Open spaces for playing fields and amenity were, compared with any precedents, very generously reserved in the plans of both towns. Experience proved, however, that in a population which is not prevented by adverse circumstances from following its natural impulse for outdoor recreation the habit expands. The appetite for space, almost literally, grows by what it feeds upon. At Letchworth in 1939, the area already in use for playing fields (public and private) and parks was 242 acres, or $13\frac{1}{8}$ acres per 1,000 inhabitants. Some part of this 242 acres will serve a larger population; but it is fair to estimate that the real need or demand for open space for recreation is not less than 10 acres per 1,000 persons, in addition to the space required for schools. Welwyn experience confirms this.

As to the location of open spaces, the theory followed in both towns was that the larger playing fields—golf courses, and football and cricket grounds—should preferably be placed towards the outer fringe of the town area, and that the smaller parks, children's

[1] I am told on good authority, though I have not checked the figures, that if, in the Duddeston-Echells redevelopment area of Birmingham, school sites were provided for that area's intended population (which is considerably less than the present population) on the standards now accepted as desirable, the whole redevelopment area would be absorbed by the school sites alone. Birmingham, however, still seems bent on getting two quarts into a pint pot.

playgrounds, tennis courts, etc., should be well dispersed throughout the central and residential areas. The theory is sound, because
it tends to reasonable concentration of the town around its centre.
In practice the theoretical arrangement has to be qualified by
such practical considerations as the contours and nature of the
land. Football and cricket grounds require level sites and good,
well-drained soil; and pieces of surviving woodland or heathland,
though usually on poor soil, are the obvious basis for major parks.
There has to be give and take between the diagrammatic logic
of economy and convenience, and the less formal logic of the
landscape. To an informed student, the balancing of these logics
gives great interest to the layout of thoughtfully developed towns
like Letchworth and Welwyn. Differences of judgment must needs
arise as to the best balance, and it is of interest that both at Letchworth and Welwyn the most intense of the local controversies on
the town plans have raged around the question of the extent to
which woodlands striking into the town area should be built upon
or preserved.

Residential Areas: Layout and Densities

Letchworth and Welwyn were meant to be, and have become,
towns for a fairly wide cross-section of British society. People of
most of the main occupational groups, including a normal proportion of the 'unoccupied' and retired, live in them. The range
of incomes is representative of all but the national extremes of
wealth and poverty. Older towns, dating from the days when
there were no income taxes and death duties, are embarrassed by
many large houses unsuited to present-day incomes and ways of
life; conversely they have many dilapidated and subdivided
dwellings in which very poor people pay rents which are small per
dwelling but high per unit of floor space. The absence of these
violent contrasts in the garden cities puzzles some visitors. It does
not seem natural that people of all grades of income should be
living in surroundings not dramatically dissimilar.

Town builders and town planners, as such, are not champions
of any particular theory as to how incomes ought to be distributed.
Their function is to cater for society as it is, or seems likely to be
in the near future. They are concerned about securing a minimum

of amenity, below which the dwellings of even the poorest should not fall; but they are not concerned with prescribing a maximum. In the two towns, anybody can have as large a house as he can afford; and sizes of building plots vary. No plot for a family house, however, may fall below the minimum considered to be essential for light, privacy and adequate garden space. This is the origin of the famous maximum density standard of twelve houses per acre, which has been imposed in both towns by the building regulations under the leases. The area for calculating this density does not include access roads; when these are included the maximum density is equivalent to about ten dwellings per 'residential acre'. There has been some elasticity in interpreting the standard. Small common gardens or greens, or minor areas usable as allotments or infants' playgrounds, are sometimes included in the calculation; and at Welwyn the standard can be averaged over a land unit up to five acres. Actually, on an individual acre here and there, are as many as fifteen houses and their gardens. But experience confirms the wisdom of the maximum of twelve houses per building acre excluding roads. It permits, and only just permits, the desired amount of privacy (from public roads and from other houses), sunlight and skylight, garden space, and variety in layout.

Generally the density, even for the smallest types of houses, falls below twelve per 'building acre'. For houses built for sale to owner-occupiers (a good test as to what people really want) the prevailing densities vary from eight down to five per 'residential acre' (including access roads); and there is a smaller, but insistent demand, for sites of a quarter to half an acre.

There is no tendency in either town towards tighter grouping; the effective demand is towards a somewhat lower average density of houses per acre with the rise in the average income of the people. The density of *persons* per acre has of course fallen more decisively with the decline in the size of the average family since Letchworth was started in 1904.*

Both towns have sought to minimize the segregation of houses of different sizes or for people of different incomes. The placing of the larger owner-occupied houses cheek by jowl with the smaller weekly-rented houses was not found popular; but groups of varying sizes of houses have been successfully placed in the same road or neighbourhood. There is less segregation of the classes than in other towns. It has been found, however, that whatever the town planner may desire, people have a marked tendency to segregate themselves by class or income. An area in which there are some noticeably large and poor families comes to be regarded as lacking in 'social tone'. The better-off tenants (whether they are clerical workers or the more highly-paid factory workers) spontaneously move to streets in which, even if the houses are no larger, the social atmosphere is regarded as superior. In the less favoured parts, rents fall, and in the more favoured parts rents rise, and this intensifies the distinction. This happened for example in Welwyn as between rented houses in parts of the south-east and the northwest areas, where the houses did not differ much in size; it was perhaps accentuated by the fact that a large group of houses in the former area, built for letting to people of medium standards of income, proved in some respects an unsatisfactory scheme. Efforts were made to improve it, but once an area loses prestige it is extremely difficult to prevent the movement from it of the better-off people to an area they like better; and the effect is of course cumulative.

It must be remembered that in a town catering for a normal cross-section of the nation, the great majority of houses—probably 75 to 80 per cent—must necessarily be houses of the council house size (having at present a floor area of from 750 to 900 square feet). The remaining 20 to 25 per cent of rather larger houses must themselves be to some extent in groups; there are hardly enough of them to leaven effectively the whole of the 75 to 80 per cent, desirable as that is in theory. With the general spread of education and culture, the avoidance of segregation by class and income may become easier. But people of like tastes and habits of life (which often, though not always, means people of appreciably equal levels of income) tend to group themselves together, whatever planners may intend and plot.

The layout of the residential groups for houses to be sold to or built on lease for owner occupiers varies in merit within each town. The estate companies themselves built a minority of houses for sale; and externally these are the best schemes, because the design of whole groups could be entrusted to single architects. The majority of houses for sale were built by speculative builders. In general speculative builders understand very well the demands of the public; but in general they, like their clients, are not good judges of architectural design. At Welwyn, a very strong control on design was maintained by the estate architect; in some parts of Letchworth the builders and their clients got their own way more completely, to the ultimate disadvantage of those clients as well as that of the town.

Council housing schemes, which form a large part of both towns, also vary in quality and design, according to the skill of the architects employed, and the degree of pressure for economy exercised by the Ministry of Health at the time. Some of the council schemes are as good as any to be found in Great Britain; others are average. None reaches the lowest depths possible to housing schemes, because there was always an estate architect to exercise some influence, though he could not always impose the standard he would desire. In both towns the council housing committees (generally representing in this the wishes of their electors) were much more conscious of internal convenience and fittings than of external appearance, and the political force behind them at times defeated the estate architects. The only remedy for this sort of unbalance is the growing public consciousness of the importance both of the internal convenience and the outside appearance of houses.*

The need of subsidiary centres in the residential areas was realized in both towns. Small subsidiary groups of shops were provided in one or two places in Letchworth, though 'neighbourhood units' in the complete sense were not at first consciously planned. The dispersal of schools, small halls, churches, tennis courts and clubrooms tended to produce some degree of neighbourhood life in certain areas; and in the post-war plans the theory is being more fully developed. At Welwyn the area east of the main railway line, owing to its separation from the main town centre by the railway itself and the factory zone, tends to become a natural 'neighbourhood', and there is a planned sub-centre containing schools, a group of shops, public halls, a public-house, and churches. But it would not I think be possible, from the experience so far gained, to state what is the correct population for a 'neighbourhood', or to say that civic consciousness will tend to gather round a part of the town rather than the town as a whole. The social structure of each of the towns is complex, and there are dozens of buildings and institutions (including the factory clubs) which are 'centres' for some aspect of it; while there is also a marked consciousness of the unity of each town as a whole, especially among the people who have lived and worked in it for a number of years.

Neighbourly association is, for deep reasons, important in the life of civilized people, but its radius is short; in a town it rarely extends beyond the dozen or score of houses nearest to one's own. Beyond that tiny geographical group, people choose their associates on the ground of particular common interest or personal attraction. Emotional, intellectual and spiritual associations do indeed arise between persons at different ends of the earth. But in a small town separated from other towns by some miles of open country, many more associations will be made by the average person within the same town than elsewhere, and his understanding of the personal inter-relationships of other people will be clearer. This it is that brings about a town's social and political unity. Intermediately, between the natural contacts arising in the group of a dozen houses and those arising in the town, there are, or could be, some 'district' or 'ward' associations on a geographical basis; and the conception of 'neighbourhoods' may be an aid to planners in placing schools, churches, groups of shops, small halls and meeting-rooms, clubs and pubs, and minor parks. But a mechanical division of the town into ring-fenced 'units' is, in my judgment, hardly practicable, since 'neighbourhoods' for these different purposes often overlap and interdigitate. Nevertheless the principle underlying the 'neighbourhood unit' idea is a good one, and will be fruitful if not over-simplified in its application.*

Chapter V

ADMINISTRATION, LOCAL GOVERN-MENT AND FINANCE

Administration: Control of Use and Appearance

Initial planning, however good, soon loses its value unless followed up by consistent and skilled management. Pope, in stating this important truth, prefaced it by an error:

> For forms of government let fools contest;
> Whate'er is best administered is best.

Sufficient yet strictly bounded powers are the raw material of good administration; and the garden city companies had such powers under their leases. But experience showed the necessity of unflagging watchfulness and strength. A case in point is the checking of the use of dwelling houses for trade. That we are a nation of would-be shopkeepers is shown by the fact that in the country as a whole one family in every baker's dozen runs a shop. On any housing estate there are constant attempts to start little shops in front parlours, besides tailoring, boot repairing, typing and all sorts of other businesses. Letchworth, at one period, was not fully alert to this tendency, and quite a number of unauthorized sweet and tobacco shops, grocery shops, haberdasheries, etc., sprang up. Once started they were difficult to get rid of, since closing them meant hardship to struggling people and the loss of a convenience (however slight) to the neighbours.

The restriction of business in dwelling houses is a matter of common sense and anticipation of the possible consequences rather than of logic. Some one-man businesses are almost inevitably carried on from private houses; I may instance the cases of doctors, dentists, veterinary surgeons and industrial insurance agents as among the least controversial. It was found necessary to have a very clear policy. Any kind of retail trade involving stocks and customers calling at the house must be nipped in the bud rigorously. And no business whatever should be just winked at; it proved essential to insist that a permit must always be applied for so that the case could be considered on its merits, and suitable conditions laid down where a permit was granted. Even in the case of professional men, a permit was not automatically granted; it was considered important to limit numbers in a profession so that each practitioner might have a fair chance of a living—at any rate when the towns were very small. In the case of such businesses as jobbing plumbers, house decorators, gardeners, window cleaners, etc., the conditions imposed covered such points as the restriction of the amount of stocks and appliances kept on the premises, the number of persons (usually not more than one) who might be employed for wages, and perhaps a prohibition on the use of the house as a workshop, and on the public advertising of the address. In certain cases a name plate or sign would be barred; in others (that of a doctor's practice for instance) a name plate of approved design would be permitted. And in granting the permit it had to be made clear that if the business grew beyond the limits laid down, the proprietor would be required to transfer it to premises in the business zone of the town; the provision of small workshops on rental was found indispensable in enforcing such rules.

The value of well administered controls in protecting the amenities of a town cannot be doubted. But they have to be handled wisely and tactfully, as well as firmly, if they are to be effective without seeming to the controlled to be pettifogging or oppressive. What is objectionable and what is permissible is not a matter of estate economics only; public sentiment must be taken into account. Thus if in a street of fifty houses there happen to be seen the name plates of one partnership of doctors, one architect, and one insurance agent, it may retain prestige as a residential street. If you add the plates of a plumber, a chimney sweep and a solicitor, six obvious businesses in fifty houses will begin to give it a 'commercial' touch. A small builder may use the telephone for business purposes from his private house, and no harm be done. But if handcarts stand outside his front gate, or a ladder commonly leans up against his garage, the atmosphere is changed. A small craftsman's workshop or an artist's studio in a back garden may seem harmless enough, but when the craftsman or artist extends his clientele, employs assistants, and branches out into allied operations involving hammering or the use of small machines, or the coming and going of a number of workers, the workshop will begin to trouble the neighbours. And if there are a dozen advertisements in the local paper inviting the public to do business with a dozen addresses in the same street, the other residents in that street will lose enthusiasm for it, even though nothing of business is visible in the street itself. It proves best for the estate to make it a rule that no business should be carried on in a private house or its out-buildings if it is practicable for it to be carried on from a recognized business area, and to judge marginal cases on their merits, while insisting always on the right of control.

The use covenants in leases of industrial premises and shops should similarly be enforced unless relaxed by express permit. The administrative difficulty in these cases is not so great. Business firms seem to resent less than private citizens the reminder that they should adhere to the agreements they have entered into.

Control of external design is a very difficult branch of administration. The powers of the garden city companies under their leases are very strong—far stronger than is likely to be exercisable by local authorities under planning schemes. Yet in the case of estate companies dictatorial rigidity is precluded by their major interest—that of securing new lessees and retaining the goodwill of existing lessees. There have been wide variations of strictness in the two towns, and at different periods within each town. It is obvious to any visitor that at Welwyn the required standards of design, and of harmony between designs, have been much higher than at Letchworth. Partly this is traceable to the dates of foundation of the towns; Letchworth had to break new ground, and the educational process started there made it a little easier for Welwyn to get the idea of architectural control accepted.

This however is not the whole explanation of the difference. The Welwyn directors undoubtedly gave higher priority to architectural design; they were prepared to support their officers in attaining it, even though it meant the occasional loss of a valuable letting. Unless an estate is prepared to face this, it cannot maintain a good aesthetic standard. But much depends also on the skill of the approving architect in judging just how far he can safely make concessions from his ideal of harmony and individual design; and he must be in close rapprochement with the letting agent, whose interest is in doing business. I record my opinion that Welwyn

was as successful as is possible in the existing state of public
opinion in securing good design of public and private buildings
under a system of free contract. There are a few estates that, over
much smaller areas, have attained an even higher standard. I do
not think so high a standard has been reached in a democratic
country in modern times over the entire area of a town.

The experience of the two towns shows that in a town centre
it is desirable to go further than to reconcile the work of different
architects by the method of approval. Closely grouped buildings
in a town centre ought to be designed as a whole by a single architect or by the collaboration of a group of architects under a
recognized leader. At Letchworth the buildings in the centre were
designed at different periods by many different architects, and
some important business streets look no better than they would
look if there had been no control at all. Welwyn has had one or
two failures—notably in its factory area—due to anxiety to con-
ciliate lessees at periods when the company could not take the
risk of offending them. But the failures are rare; the prevailing
standard is quite astonishingly high. If relatively I criticize the
architectural control at Letchworth, I must again remind the
reader that Letchworth was the first complete town in modern
times to attempt control of design at all, that such control
was repugnant to public opinion, that the very idea of it had to
win its way.

Control of extensions or alterations to existing buildings proved
a matter requiring much firmness and tact. On occasion drastic
action has to be taken if the control is not to become a dead letter.
At Welwyn one or two lessees had to be asked to remove un-
sanctioned additions, and became enemies of the estate company
for life. The difficulty is at its greatest in the case of urgently
required extensions to industrial buildings; and in their factory
areas both towns show examples of successful pressure against the
better judgment of their architects.

My experience when estate manager of Welwyn was that control
had always to be sympathetically exercised, but became easier as
time went on, and the character of the town became established
and recognized. Public taste improved, and protests against lax
consents were useful as a counterweight to the far more frequent
and intense resistances to control. Architects who had designed

buildings for clients were sometimes the most embittered opponents; indeed I cannot say that architects, though critical of lapses, were an influence supporting aesthetic control as a whole. The subject is inherently a difficult one. The individual client wants individuality; and the architect wants to materialize his commission in any given case, even though in theory he supports harmony. An estate management always has an interest in doing business and pleasing its customers. An estate architect, under pressure from two sides, is all too human. So in practice there is more danger of laxity than of aesthetic tyranny. The natural pressure of lay opinion is towards laxity. It would be a good thing therefore if every town had some sort of civic society or planning group to hold up the end of planning and architectural control, and to educate the public in appreciation of design. Such a body would encourage the estate management or planning committee in a reasonable degree of firmness, and help it to face a sectional outcry when some dearly desired atrocity is turned down.

Conflicts and changes in architectural style created another intractable problem. 'Modernist' architects whose designs were rejected as clashing with a 'traditionalist' street or group did not hesitate to accuse the estate architects of being obstacles to progress. On the other hand, the incursion of non-traditional designs in certain areas was rightly criticized as clashing with the established harmony. Welwyn has held to the view that, while there is no need for a town to be all in one style, there must be harmony in groups seen as a whole. But there is room for difference of judgment as to what is the appropriate 'group'. Behind the whole problem is the fact that many people who like good design in individual buildings, dislike uniformity in the buildings in a road; while some want to own buildings which stand out conspicuously from the rest and will not come to a town which discourages that ambition.

In both towns the estate architects preferred the building of the smaller houses in terraces or blocks, these terraces being themselves fairly closely grouped to give harmonious town effects;[1] prospective purchasers, on the contrary, always preferred detached or semi-detached houses, and short-term tenants fought hard to get

[1] Sir Raymond Unwin was the leading modern advocate of this principle: see *Town Planning in Practice* (1909).

the end houses of terrace blocks. Many experiments were made to find the forms of layout that would best reconcile the points of view of architects and occupiers. Where costs had to be cut to the bone, the solution was usually in the form of blocks of four to six houses, arranged in streets, closes, and squares, and sometimes around greens in crescent shape. Where there was a little money to spare, individuality and privacy were married to architectural harmony and continuity by linking walls and the careful placing of garages. Trellis screens were also extensively used; and planting and landscape gardening often played an integral part in group design. I can testify, after persistent trials, that it was almost impossible to *sell* a house in the middle of a block, however well designed; and even in the case of houses for letting the rents of the centre houses had to be lower than those at the ends—such is the strength of popular feeling in all classes in favour of the house having at least three free walls. The architectural problem thus presented cannot I feel be inherently insoluble; and architects who base their theory of aesthetics on the functional principle should be the last to seek to evade a solution which will meet the clients' requirements. In any case you cannot steam-roller the public to make things easier for architects.

Advertising on residential premises is difficult to control, as it often begins by small trade cards and 'temporary' notices. These have to be objected to at once, and public opinion supports firmness in this case. Not so with posters advertising meetings and other events. In both towns some latitude had to be allowed for these, so long as they were occasional and were removed when the event had passed. Permanent poster boards in private gardens, containing religious or political slogans, are more objectionable, and neighbours were found to uphold their prohibition provided it was impartial as between parties and sects. In both towns the check on posters on houses is aided by the fact that there are public notice boards in key positions, and that otherwise hoardings and poster advertising are almost wholly barred. (Letchworth has one hoarding for large commercial posters in its town centre.) Keeping the public notice boards in decent condition is important, and not easy; there have been times in both towns when they were something of a blot on the landscape, though always a strictly localized blot.

Sheds, fowl houses, rabbit pens, amateur-designed porches, unauthorized trellises, etc., require the constant vigilance of the administration. They can spread like a rash, and once established are difficult to clean up. In the case of weekly rented houses the co-operation of the housing managers is indispensable. It is important not to let any structure go unnoticed, but to insist on application for a permit in every case. Conditions can then be imposed: as for example, in the case of a chicken house, that the number of birds shall be within a certain limit, that cockerels shall be barred, and that the structure shall be of pleasing or at least inoffensive design. The size and density of planting of gardens must be taken into account, and the position of every outbuilding studied in relation to its appearance from neighbouring houses. In both towns, consents are necessarily often refused, and public opinion increasingly supports a careful control. During the war, however, the former rigidity has been much relaxed. Whatever may be the degree of toleration of the appearance of outbuildings, it is essential to insist on rules which will prevent noise, smell and the breeding of rats and other vermin.

Enforcing the proper care of gardens and hedges is, in the case of the smaller houses, a matter more easily undertaken by the housing estate managements within the town than by the town administration directly. It is very difficult to insist on a rigid standard. The majority of occupiers are so interested in their own amenities as to require no outside stimulus. The proportion who neglect gardens and hedges to the extent of producing eyesores offensive to others is very small; maybe 5 to 8 per cent. In the case of back gardens it is not necessary to be very strict; and in fact action is not taken unless there is a crop of weeds threatening the neighbouring plots. Front gardens matter more, and in rare cases management pressure has to be exercised. Welwyn found it best that the housing managements should themselves clip and maintain the front hedges. This produces a general well-kept appearance, within which the few lapses from a good standard of private gardening do not matter so much. There are cases in both towns where front gardens are unfenced, and looked after by the housing management or the estate, sometimes with the aid of a committee of tenants of the group.*

Alongside the railway lines, which run through the centres of both estates, amenities were found to need special attention. The problem is less obtrusive at Letchworth, where a double line lies largely in cutting, than at Welwyn, where six tracks, as well as a large goods yard, bisect the town. In both cases the railway land, and the buildings thereon, are outside the estate control. There was some consultation between the railway company's engineers and the estate architects as to the design of the station buildings; and at Welwyn the main building is in a style consistent with the 'neo-Georgian' business street in which it stands. Goods sheds and bridges however (especially at Welwyn) are 'functional' to an inconsiderate degree; and the commercial advertising department of the railway has allowed posters on the stations without much restraint or skill in placing. The railway company, fortunately, is showing increasing interest in amenities; and at Welwyn there has recently been set up a joint standing committee of the L.N.E.R., the U.D.C., and the Welwyn company, to consider what can be done about the planting and amenities of the station and railway land, including the sidings—a most useful precedent for other towns. It is fair to say that both at Letchworth and Welwyn the railway company could make some case for the improvement of the appearance of one or two factories as seen by their passengers from the line.*

Noise and smoke have not been much of a problem in either town. Most of the factories are driven by electric power, and any tendency for the emission of black smoke (as for example from heating installations) is kept in check by a county byelaw. The houses being modern, the types of fireplaces used are not the worst, and the low density and great amount of tree planting makes the smoke factor virtually negligible. The factories having heavy machinery producing noise are few and so placed that they are not a nuisance. At Welwyn, church and school calling bells were disallowed under the leases; and factory hooters (those brutal and nowadays unnecessary reminders of time-slavery) were only in fashion during the air-raid period when they were put in as part of the public warning system. Smells from chemical processes occasionally evidenced themselves, but the powers under the leases enabled them to be controlled.

Local Government

The creation of the two towns led to changes in the local government set-up of their areas. Originally the Letchworth estate consisted of parts of three parishes, all in the same rural district. The Welwyn estate consisted of parts of four parishes, in three different rural districts. In its fourth year Letchworth was created a separate civil parish. The same step was taken at Welwyn in its first year, the rural district boundaries being revised so that the new parish was wholly within one rural district. For some years each town had a Parish Council and was also represented on the Rural District Council. Most of what are normally regarded as public services were at this stage undertaken by the estate companies—notably road maintenance, street lighting, sewage disposal, and water supply; charges being leviable (and at Letchworth actually levied) for these services under special covenants of the leases. Letchworth attained the status of an Urban District in its fifteenth year (1919) when its population was 10,000. Welwyn became an Urban District in its sixth year (1926) when its population was only 4,077. The rateable values at this stage were: Letchworth £67,158; Welwyn £38,975.

During the Parish Council phase at Welwyn, the little used machinery of a Parochial Committee was set up, the body consisting of the members of the Parish Council and the parish representatives on the R.D.C. The parish was made a separate rating area, and this enabled the R.D.C. to sponsor an active housing policy, to take over new roads (frontage charges being levied on the rates and not on frontagers as such), and to provide street lighting, without placing any burden on the rest of the rural district.

Later, both at Letchworth and Welwyn, the Urban District Councils took over responsibility for sewage disposal. At Letchworth the water supply is still provided by the company, and charged for under the leases; at Welwyn the U.D.C. has taken over this service. Neither Council owns the gas or electricity services; at Letchworth both are run by the estate company; at Welwyn the company takes electricity in bulk from the Northmet Company and has its own distribution subsidiary, while gas is provided by a statutory company by way of high-pressure mains to a gas-holder on the estate.*

Both Urban District Councils now take the main responsibility for low-cost housing. Both play an ever-increasing part in development, and are in close and continuous contact with the estate companies. Co-operation has been good throughout, and though from time to time differences of opinion arise on specific points, there has never been acute tension. In the early years several persons served both on the boards of the companies and as elected councillors, and this assisted co-ordination, though it also provided occasion for criticism by puristic citizens. At Welwyn, from 1921 up to 1934, three Civic Directors of the Company were appointed by the Parish Council or Urban District Council; and during the same period executives of the estate company functioned also as the chief officers (Clerk, Rating and Finance Officer, and Engineer-Surveyor) of the Council. Since then full-time officers have been appointed.

The Hertfordshire County Council were from the start reasonably co-operative. They had to be cautious in committing themselves to expenditure on county services (schools for instance) in the new towns while their future seemed speculative. Indeed they had no power to provide such services in anticipation of demand —which was what was really required in order to get the towns established as quickly as possible. But their chief officers took a real interest in the new towns and followed as liberal a policy as they could in fulfilling their statutory responsibilities.

Statutory planning schemes under the Town and Country Planning Acts were not begun for the two towns until quite recently. In each case the Urban District Council is the planning authority, but as the plans of the companies were in advance of any scheme which the Councils could impose, it was agreed that the companies' plans should be deposited with the Councils, with an undertaking not to vary from them without notice and consultation. Now that Town and Country Planning is compulsory for all areas, statutory schemes are being proposed on the basis of the companies' plans; and for all development consent has to be obtained from the Councils under Interim Development Procedure as well as from the companies under their leases. It remains to be seen whether this dual planning control will produce as good planning as is possible under the enlightened single administration of a leasehold estate. I must confess that I doubt it. But the problem remains as to how the advantages of unitary ownership under free enterprise can be united with consistency in service of the public interest. Nor must we overlook the problem as to how we can protect ourselves against bureaucratic tyranny under unified land ownership, whether public or private.*

Garden City Finance: Housing Subsidies

I have already referred to the predominant financial problem of the two garden city companies in their early years: a chronic starvation of capital. When you look at their resources and the commitments they started with, it seems astonishing that they succeeded in getting going at all. This brings to light a rather surprising fact: that it does not require a vast amount of risk-taking share capital to build a town. The enterprise differs radically from a manufacturing or trading business, in that capital values of a stable character are produced as money is spent, and if the expenditure is on a sound plan, these values come to show a surplus over direct cost. On the other hand, if a large part of the capital for development has to be borrowed at fixed rates of interest (which becomes possible because the increase of capital value provides demonstrable security) the compound interest on borrowed money will exceed, for a while, the actual revenue from new development. In this typical situation there are two possible methods of accounting. Either the shortfall can be treated as a revenue loss; or it can be added to the capital investment—the addition being justified by valuations of the estate on a capital basis. Broadly speaking, Letchworth followed the former method, Welwyn the latter. Each has its drawbacks; treating the inevitable shortfall in the first years as a revenue loss dries up the sources of investment capital; whereas capitalizing it involves the risk that at some point loan capital may dry up too, owing to the delay in covering the annual charges by realized revenues. A better answer than either would be to raise ample equity capital at the start, since in the nature of the case there must be some interval before revenue fully covers charges on capital, and equity capital expects to wait for its full return; but for the reasons given, this answer was not available to either garden city company.

Compared with a trading or manufacturing concern, a property

company can, with financial wisdom, be much more 'highly
geared' (that is its fixed-interest-bearing capital can safely be
relatively high in proportion to its equity capital), because ground
rent revenues, once created, are of almost 'gilt edged' stability.
Nevertheless, I think it must be admitted that, even for property
companies, Letchworth and Welwyn became too highly geared.
At Letchworth the shareholders had to wait too long (twenty
years) for their modest 5 per cent per annum; it is a paradox, but
true, that with the same rate of growth but with more share capital
the full 5 per cent would have been paid earlier and arrears overtaken sooner. Moreover the capital appreciation of the Letchworth estate has not been brought fully into the company's
accounts by up-to-date valuations. Welwyn grew more rapidly,
but its original development expenditure had to be financed
largely by debentures and bonds at fixed rates of 6 to 7 per cent
per annum. The capitalization of this interest was covered by
expert valuations of the estate, but compound interest at these
high rates delayed too long the crossing of the vital curves of
revenue and interest, and at a reconstruction in 1934 the capital
was reduced by £375,000.

A notable episode in the financial history of Welwyn was the
experiment in governmental finance. Under a section of the
Housing Act, 1921 (since re-enacted as section 35 of the Town and
Country Planning Act 1932) powers were given to the Public
Works Loan Commissioners to make loans to an authorized association 'for the purpose of developing a garden city'. To qualify
for such loans the authorized association had to have a limit on
its dividends, which at the time was fixed by the Treasury at 7 per
cent per annum; and the loans were not to exceed 75 per cent of
a Government valuation and were to be secured by a mortgage.
The Welwyn company applied for and obtained loans under this
provision between 1921 and 1930. But the partnership did not
prove a happy one. The Government valuations were far lower
than the independent expert valuations of the estate; the loans
had to be repaid over thirty years; the rate of interest was at first
5½ per cent, though it declined to 4¾ per cent on subsequent loans;
a limit of £300,000 was placed on the total advances, which was
not enough to suit the case; and some extremely inconvenient, and
I think unnecessary, conditions were imposed. The company

could have done as well, or better, by borrowing in the open market; and after strenuous efforts to get the system improved, it finally repaid the loans and replaced them by private mortgages.

It is arguable that the creation of new towns, being a social enterprise affecting the welfare of people over future centuries, should not be judged by immediate financial considerations at all—that it is more analogous to afforestation, on which the return is so long delayed that only the state can undertake it. Rightly, or wrongly, however, Howard and the garden city companies set out in the belief that even so great a scheme could be, and ought to be, a business proposition. In this they reflected what Emerson described as one of the English traits: 'The Crystal Palace is not considered honest unless it pays; no matter how much convenience, beauty, or *éclat*, it must be self-supporting.' How far have the two garden cities proved themselves 'honest' in this austere sense?

Both companies are now paying a regular 5 per cent on their share capital, and Letchworth is gradually catching up its arrears of cumulative dividend. Neither can be said to have fulfilled the financial hopes of shareholders, and in the case of Welwyn, some part of the fixed-interest capital, as well as the share capital, suffered a reduction in the reconstruction of 1934. Yet both have attained a really strong position. They have little difficulty now in raising, by means of loans secured on their substantial assets, the further capital needed for development; nor in covering new expenditure out of quickly realized additional revenue. And the true present value of the estates may well be sufficient to cover all past development costs (including administrative overheads), plus compound interest from the start, at rates now considered appropriate to the character of the security. Welwyn was specially unlucky in being compelled to shoulder initial development expenditure in 1920-1, when costs were inflated and the rate of interest, even on gilt-edged securities, as high as 6 per cent. Given a somewhat quicker rate of development, or a somewhat lower rate of interest, both Letchworth and Welwyn would have paid up their cumulative dividends and produced a surplus years ago.*

The fundamental basis of garden city building, as a business, is the conversion of undeveloped land, having an agricultural value as low as from £1 to £4 per acre per annum, into urban land with a much higher annual value, realized gradually in the creation of ground rents as sites are leased for actual building. The ground rents obtainable bear little or no relationship to the cost of production; they depend on what the owners (and ultimately the occupiers) of the different classes of buildings are willing to pay. The cost of production of a building site is represented by the initial purchase price of the land plus the cost of the roads, sewers and other capital works necessary to turn it into a building site; and in addition the overhead expenses of planning, administration and such unremunerative services as sewage outfall works, estate maintenance, gardening, and initial amenities, are part of the true cost of production, which must (if the business is to be sound) finally be covered out of the revenues of the estate. It is a matter of subtle analysis and judgment, however, as to how these overhead costs are to be charged out on different types of development. If for example the expenses over the whole period of development were to be charged out to all sites built on in proportion to rental values realized, the sites of small houses of the Council housing class would show a heavy loss, and the sites of middle-class and larger houses and of factories would show little or no profit. It is on the sites for shops and other commercial premises only that any big surplus over cost is to be expected, and a greater speed than either Letchworth or Welwyn attained is needed if the surplus on commercial sites is to counterbalance the loss on housing sites. Land development however was not the only business and source of revenue in either case. The Letchworth accounts benefited very substantially by the company's water, gas and electricity undertakings, though it engaged in very little building of any kind. The Welwyn accounts benefited by a successful electricity undertaking and remunerative investments in shops and factory buildings; the company's investments in housing on the whole covered their charges; but some of its other subsidiary enterprises showed deficits for a considerable period. In both towns recent expenditure on development, and in the case of Welwyn on business buildings, shows a return more than sufficient to cover charges on borrowings for the purpose, and as the towns grow in population the percentage surplus on new investment is certain to increase.

Town building is a long-term enterprise, and both schemes were intended to have permanent public value as well as to produce a moderate return for the investors. Letchworth retains in its constitution Howard's basic principle that, after the payment of the cumulative 5 per cent on shares, surplus revenues must be used for the benefit of the town. The inhabitants thus own, in effect, the equity of the estate; and in years to come this will prove of great importance. I must express my personal view that it is regrettable that the inhabitants of Welwyn, when the company was reconstructed, lost this equity. Not only was this a departure from the original idea, but I do not believe it was in the long run in the interests of the company, since its monopoly position as owner of the entire freehold must in time create fears of exploitation and tend to check the enthusiastic support of the business interests and residents who have a stake in the town; or alternatively must lead to an irresistible demand for the public ownership of the estate. Because I see many advantages in control by a body free of party politics and bureaucracy, I feel the right solution is the restoration, in some form, of the public equity. I must add, however, quite categorically, that so far there has not been the slightest sign of exploitation or abuse of the company's position; on the contrary, the tradition that it has public responsibility has been fully maintained.

In assessing the financial results of town building, it should be borne in mind that the share capital of the estate companies is only a small fraction of the total capital employed. Far larger sums have been invested in houses, factories and other buildings than in the land and land development; and on these, in general, a normal return has been paid. If you compare the finance of housing in these two towns with that of housing in a typical overcrowded city centre, the public economy of the garden-city method is so great as to dwarf the partial writing-off of Welwyn's private capital or the arrears of dividend of Letchworth.

Look for example at the public cost of Welwyn housing. From 1920 to 1938, 2,742 houses were built there under the Housing Acts. Of these 1,518 received Exchequer subsidies, of a capitalized value of about £200,000. Under the Housing Act of 1938 the cost of Exchequer subsidies on 2,742 houses on expensive sites in city centres was estimated at £41,130 per annum for forty years—equivalent at twenty-two years' purchase to over £900,000. Really this comparison minimizes the difference, since in 1938 contemporary schemes in the garden cities were entitled to no Exchequer

ADMINISTRATION, LOCAL GOVERNMENT, FINANCE

subsidies at all. But even on this basis the total capital write-off at Welwyn, adding the Exchequer's £200,000 to the private investors' £375,000, comes to £575,000, against a £900,000 loss to the Exchequer on the same amount of housing in the centres of big cities, on standards socially far less satisfactory. When the local rate subsidies are taken into account, the contrast is even more striking. On the same number of houses the capitalized value of the contribution from local rates in a case of expensive sites comes to £450,000. The actual cost to the Welwyn rates may be roughly capitalized at £25,000.

Advocates of garden-city building have repeatedly protested against this differentiation of the national subsidies. Clearly it encourages the undue concentration of dwellings and workplaces in big cities. If rates of subsidy are differentiated at all, the scale should be loaded in favour of, not against, planned relocation centres. If the garden cities had received housing subsidies at the same rates as redevelopment areas, they could have let their houses at lower rents, or built better houses at the prevailing rents, and would thereby have attracted industry and population more quickly—to the national advantage. It seems to me outrageous that replacement housing—which adds less to national assets—should have been subsidized by the State more generously than new development. Differential subsidies might have been justified as an instrument of national policy designed to steer industry and population where it was desirable they should go. The policy of successive Ministries of Health did the exact opposite; it steered industry and population to the most disadvantageous situations.

Of course the official case for the 1938 type of subsidy was that it was necessary, to enable the authorities of great cities to rehouse the overcrowded and to clear slums. But when the rehousing took the form of centrally situated flats, the subsidy really went towards paying high prices for land (incidentally driving values still higher). When it took the form of suburban housing schemes, the subsidy became in effect a grant towards the workers' cost of travel to city centres, thus facilitating the continued location in those centres of workplaces which might otherwise have been impelled to move out. In both cases the economic effect of the subsidy was to promote the concentration and expansion of big cities.

What was overlooked entirely was that housing in garden cities was really an alternative way, and a better way, of rehousing overcrowded populations, or of avoiding the further development of overcrowded populations. True, the individuals housed were not identifiable as coming from or being helped out of particular congested areas. But whenever an industry chose to settle in one of the new towns, it had before it the alternative of settling in a big city; in some few cases firms actually moved out along with their personnel. If a firm had elected to go to an overcrowded centre, thereby increasing the pressure on local living space, the Exchequer would in due course have subsidized heavily the rents of its workers' houses when built to relieve the pressure. But if the firm chose to go to one of the new towns, and so refrained from increasing the congestion problem, little or no subsidy was available for its workers' houses. It is hard to conceive a more witless discrimination.

To sum up the financial experience. Letchworth and Welwyn certainly did not yield a full commercial return to their equity shareholders; but they came near enough to doing so to show that with adequate initial capital and a greater pace of growth they would have been financial successes in this sense. On a broad view, taking public and private investments together, they made a better showing than development near the centres or on the fringes of congested cities. Not only have they drawn less on State grants, but they have also been quite exceptionally independent of private charity. The churches, public buildings, open spaces and other amenities of most of the older towns have largely been provided by gifts and bequests of the wealthy. The garden cities have almost wholly paid for their amenities themselves; and of the millions of pounds spent on their buildings and development, all but a marginal sum has earned a full commercial return. And this in spite of the fact that the garden cities, as pioneer enterprises, swam against the stream of developmental fashion and public policy. To-day the value of the assets of the two companies is, I feel sure, more than sufficient to cover the whole of the capital invested plus compound interest at rates now accepted as normal. If the two companies had not been stinted of capital, or if fashion in industrial location had changed a little sooner, or if there had been some measure of canalization of development towards dispersal centres under a national planning policy, the financial success of the garden cities would have required no qualification at all.

Chapter VI

SOCIAL LIFE AND CULTURE

I am conscious of the difficulty, in a short section, of characterizing the social atmosphere of the garden cities. Where two or three gather together, there is society; and the permutations and combinations of social grouping in the smallest of towns are so infinitely complex that to describe them would be like writing thousands of biographies in one. There are ways in which intelligible and partially true impressions might be conveyed to a reader; for example by skilled sociological surveys supported (and necessarily dehumanized) by masses of statistics; or by a series of novels of Balzacian or Proustian amplitude. A novel about life in a town, written by a resident genius of wide sympathy and power of observation, could transmit facets of the truth—but it would be one person's distillation from millions of impressions; and in fact the best of such novels is rarely accepted by contemporary citizens as a balanced picture of a community. Survey reports, based on collected testimonies from sample inhabitants answering questionnaires, represent the constituents of reality much as dehydrated egg-powder represents eggs; in fact less truly (even if flavour is thought not to matter), because they can be no more than assemblies of the unreflecting momentary impressions of a percentage of mute inglorious Balzacs and Prousts. Of the two, I would prefer the novels; but though many novelists have lived in our two towns, a good novel of life in either of them has still to come; and when it does come it will probably tell us a lot more about the author than about his fellow citizens at large.

I am not so foolish therefore as to think I can, in these paragraphs, justly and completely portray the social life of Letchworth and Welwyn. What I say is designed to do little more than correct ill-informed outside assessments or guesses, and to point to a few things about the towns that seem to me distinctive. I lived in Letchworth for five years, when its population was growing from 8,000 to 12,500; subsequently I have retained contact with a number of people there, have read the local newspaper regularly, and have visited the town frequently. I have lived at Welwyn for twenty-five years while it has grown from zero—even zero stands for a rural population of 400—to about 18,000. I have encountered, talked with, and joined in doing many different things with some thousands of people in these towns; I have been specially interested in their goings on; but of course I have had my own purposes, hopes and wishes, which necessarily colour my judgment. I feel I have in my mind's eye as comprehensive a picture of the social structure of the two towns as one person is likely to have. Yet when I sit down to reflect upon and summarize what I know I realize that any such picture is composed rather than photographic. In a small town one knows far more people in the round, by direct contact and by others' opinions of them, than one does in a big city; but still one intimately knows only a minority; and one's conception is really built up by generalizing from observed ways of life that one judges to be typical of many others. As I formulate my impressions I tend to forget how relatively limited my basic data are—and especially in how few of the groupings and associations of my fellow citizens I have had a continuous part. The reader may do well to bear this in mind.

I start with one fairly confident generalization. The fundamental shape of most people's lives in the garden cities resembles that in other English cities and towns. The inhabitants came mostly from places (urban and rural) in the London and Home Counties region; a biggish minority from other parts of Great Britain, including Scotland and Wales; a few from continental countries; and a fraction from the United States. Though small, the foreign leaven is important, because it mainly consists of people in executive positions in specialized industries. But Southern English ways set the general character. Since younger people more readily move to new settlements, the average age (especially at Welwyn, the newer town) is below that of the nation as a whole; but not remarkably so, because the towns also attract a certain number of retired people. Compared with older country towns of like size, the garden cities have more people of enterprise, originality, social energy; one explanation of which is that both towns are centres of modern and expanding industries, some of them of 'scientific' character.

In the main the employed people in the garden cities came to

them because they obtained jobs there; some got jobs there because
the living conditions appealed to them, but these were a very small
minority. The 'dormitory' or 'season ticket' element is negligible
at Letchworth. At Welwyn it amounts to 15 per cent, and these
residents came to the town because they liked it, or at least liked
the houses they could get in it; they work mostly in London
offices. Some workers employed in both garden cities live in the
villages and towns nearby. At Welwyn these (I give 1939 figures)
about balance those who live in the town and work in London; at
Letchworth the proportion who come in to work is larger.*

The social composition that results is not far from an average
cross-section of the functional and income groups of urban Great
Britain as a whole. Extremes, I think, are relatively absent. There
are no local millionaires; while the ultra-depressed to be found in
the slum quarters of great cities, who scratch a living in dubious
and chancy ways, are under-represented. Welwyn's 15 per cent
of London black-coated workers, added to those of the same stra-
tum working locally, give the town a 'middle class' numerically
in excess of the national average; this has proved important
socially and culturally, but their numbers are not enough to make
Welwyn primarily a 'middle-class enclave'. Both garden cities are
predominantly manufacturing towns, with the social composition
of manufacturing towns. Quite half the working population—
more than half at Letchworth—find their work in the factories,
and most of the rest in the local shops, trades, services and professions. While the great majority are weekly wage earners and
their families, it must not be overlooked that in modern industry
the number of working directors, managers, executives and highly
paid technicians is substantial. More of these live on the spot at
Letchworth, and many more at Welwyn, than in an ordinary
industrial town—relatively few diffuse themselves in the surrounding countryside—and their presence is a source of social strength.
Like all 'middle classes' these groups undertake more than their
mathematical quota of cultural leadership and public welfare
work.

A visitor from Mars or Moscow would no doubt be struck more
by the similarities of life in the two towns to that in other English
towns than by the differences. Looked at with alien eyes, the
differences are marginal. And yet to a closer observer it is just the

variations from the standard that are interesting. One source of the distinctive character of the garden cities is that at no distant date they were pioneer communities. A small but growing number of people, mostly of urban habits, found themselves thrown together, strangers to each other, and greater strangers to the scattered rural population whose land they were invading. They were of all classes: a few technicians concerned in development, a larger number of building workers, and gradually an addition of specialists and workers engaged in the first services of the community, and of adventurous souls attracted by the idea of taking part in creating a new town, and having houses built for themselves there.

The group being so mixed, it might be supposed that any sort of social 'getting together' would be difficult. The contrary proved the case. Social energy was released at its highest power; barriers of class and income were for the time being ignored. This was not because people had undergone a spiritual change; it was simply that under conditions of such close contact snobbish distinctions would have appeared so blatantly in bad taste that they were impracticable. Everybody without exception went to the same meetings and functions, to the same religious meetings, political discussions, dances, social gatherings, tennis parties, amateur plays, impromptu concerts. The first wedding, the first christening, the first funeral, the first event organized by some new society (and new societies sprang up at the rate of one a week), were matters of at least curious interest to all. There was no established social hierarchy to thwart people's spontaneous friendliness—nobody who by traditional right must be asked to be chairman or secretary of anything. The Admirable Crichton pulled his weight without the shadow of an impending rescue to put him back in his place. In the British people (as Barrie's play illustrates) a native democratic sentiment struggles always against the technical and political forces making for stratification; in the primitive community of a garden city in its early phase the democratic impulse had full rein. Everybody liked the atmosphere created, and the experience coloured the future when the normal complexity of society began to develop.

I did not see this pioneering phase at Letchworth; when I arrived there in its eighth year I heard a great deal about it from earlier residents who pitied me for having missed the golden age. At Welwyn I went right through it, and now therefore understand what they meant. In both towns, it may be, the surviving pioneers somewhat glorify their recollections and fancy they were happier than in fact they were. They do recall, however, that they had hardships to put up with: waddling about in gumboots because of the prevalence of mud; no shops other than a temporary general store; lighting and cooking by oil lamps; and even the intense social life limited by one army hut which was at the same time the school, the church, the council chamber, the dance hall and concert room and public forum. At Welwyn I had the official job of dealing with grumbles and endeavouring to explain away the defects of the primitive communal equipment; and I therefore remember better than most that one of the popular sports of that energetic democracy was sticking pins into the estate management. Yet I too feel it was among the best of many happy times. As the towns grew, ring-fenced social groups tended to appear. Snobbery and class distinction, dislikeable as I find them, have real and deep roots in the ways of life engendered by different functions, kinds of work, incomes, and educational backgrounds. They exist in the garden cities; they may develop further. But I doubt if they will ever reach the level usual in towns whose social structure was formed in a less 'democratic' age. The tradition of the two towns is strongly against social exclusiveness. To me this is a congenial bias; it may not be so to all. The attitudes set in the pioneering days are likely, I think, to have permanent influence; at any rate their influence has survived to date.

Common to the social life of both towns is the background of a decent home for virtually every family, and of local employment for most. At all times and everywhere the main interests of settled people, unless thwarted by environmental conditions, revolve around their homes, and to a less but important extent around their daily occupations. The fact that on the whole people live within a few minutes of their work adds to effective leisure time considerably.[1] Community life expands outward from the home life and the factory life; only for the small percentage of the foot-loose (for example some of the single folks living in lodgings) is

---

[1] Inter-factory league cricket matches are, for example, often played in the evenings—an innings per evening on two successive days.

community life, or commercial entertainment, an indispensable substitute for family life. It follows that the amount of time the inhabitants devote to fortuitous assembly in the streets, restaurants and places of entertainment tends to be less than in a city where dwellings are cramped and unattractive and hold little emotional or cultural interest. Let me not exaggerate this difference; even in the biggest city—even in Paris, where the life of the cafés and boulevards seems to dominate everything—the mass of people, and especially the lower-paid workers, centre their leisure lives round their homes or nowhere; though, alas, those who have no centre at all are all too numerous.[1] Still, it is a fact that the good homes in the garden cities do appreciably reduce the habit of casual foregathering and the demand for pay-at-the-door types of entertainment. Enthusiastic politicians complain that it is difficult to hold an open-air meeting in a garden city; too few people are wandering about at a loss for something to do. A transient resident or visitor is apt to misinterpret this; there seems to be less going on, there are fewer things one can do on the spur of the moment, than in an older city. The observation is, I think, correct; but the explanation is not social deadness, but a different and in truth more active form of social life.

Certainly the garden cities do not begin to compare with the big cities in the variety of commercial and professional entertainment they sustain locally. This I think may be true even in ratio to population. If it is a drawback (and for many people used to life in big cities it is) time and growth can remedy it; indeed the target populations of 35,000 to 50,000 were fixed to make possible a reasonable range of this class of amenities along with the rest. But it is an interesting point, which the garden cities now have to consider, whether the development of commercial entertainment up to the limit of the local possibilities would in fact produce the most satisfying culture. They can go this way if they choose, yet it would be a pity if in doing so they lost their present intensity of community life and the rich and varied culture that is based on voluntary impulse and association. There is, I believe, a sort

---

[1] Think, for instance, of the essential homelessness of the Parisian types in Balzac's *Père Goriot*, or in Jules Romain's *Les Hommes de Bonne Volonté*, or for a recent London example, of the people in Patrick Hamilton's *Twenty Thousand Streets under the Sky*.

of 'Gresham's law' of culture; just as bad money drives out good, so can a plethora of cheap passive entertainment drive out individual and associational creativeness. Personal participation in the activities of a geographical community adds incalculably to the fulness of life. Because it has aspects of responsibility as well as of privilege, some people who have known nothing but an atomized existence in great cities tend to be scared of the test of community life; but by almost everybody the latter is preferred when both have been experienced.

In broad character the social and cultural activities in the garden cities are those common to British people in any situation where the physical facilities exist. Outdoor sports take a large place, especially among the younger people, and they are of all the well-known types—football, golf, cricket, tennis, squash, badminton, riding, fencing, fishing, rambling, cycling, etc.—and of course for these the opportunities are exceptionally good and are available to virtually all ranges of income. Horticultural, animal-keeping, and food-producing societies represent another big group of interests. Societies for drama, music, and the visual arts are numerous. In Welwyn, for example, there are always four or five regular dramatic societies, each with a character of its own, besides many groups which produce plays occasionally; and around these has gathered an interchangeable pool of producers, playwrights, scene designers, stage craftsmen and electricians, and musicians, as well as of actors and actresses. The annual Welwyn Drama Festival, held for ten years up to 1939, but suspended during the war, drew competing teams from all over England and attained standards of real distinction. The musical circles range from orchestras and choirs, societies and clubs for serious music, to popular orchestras and dance bands—the last, as elsewhere, being usually part-time professionals. Dancing is a most important activity; ballroom dances are held with great frequency in many halls in both towns, while tap dancing, ballet dancing, 'keep fit' gymnastics and folk dancing find popularity with special groups. Indoor games, among them bridge, whist, chess and darts, have of course many devotees. Political meetings are incessant; the level of political interest and discussion in both towns is high. Innumerable specialized societies give public platforms to speakers on every conceivable subject. There are many 'youth' organizations. All the religious bodies are represented, from the Churches of England and Rome to the Salvation Army and Christian Science—the two older communions, the Society of Friends and the Free Churches being particularly strong. There are in fact organizations for all interests from industry, business, and trade unionism, through health and public welfare services, to the graces of life—literature, history, languages, science, handicrafts and hobbies. A notable feature of this wealth of societies is that many of them gather round factory life; to me this is significant; it shows that where the factory atmosphere is good people in general have no strong desire to escape in their leisure time from those with whom they are associated in their working hours.

It is an old joke in both towns that there is a society and a half to every man, woman and child. Now there are, I know, critics who look down on all this voluntary group activity as a poor affair beside the complex of professional arts and entertainments collected in the larger cities. As a culture, are not its standards of attainment too low to interest persons of developed taste? Indeed, does it deserve the name of culture at all? I think it does, that in fact it is a high culture; but I want to make clear where its strength does and does not lie. It does not lie in a uniformly brilliant level of *expertise*; though, as in all cultures, high spots appear intermittently. Thus, for instance, the cricket and football played by garden city teams is not quite up to the standard of the games watched by metropolitan crowds deprived of play-space for themselves. This, however, does not make the games less interesting even to watch; the drama of the contest is the same; the spectators are not less enthralled because they know the players personally rather than by character studies in the Sunday papers. The standard of play is a good standard, as it will always be where playing-fields are good, and where enough people make the game a main leisure interest. From a background of this kind a first-class player will at times emerge; he may or may not become a professional. But obviously, if the cream of the clubs of Britain is drawn off to form teams who play in the big centres, those teams must achieve a more expert ensemble.

It is the same with other forms of culture. The acting, the orchestral playing, the singing, the boxing, the billiards, the painting, even the flower and vegetable growing, to be seen at garden city events are, on the average, of higher standard than will be found at the equivalent amateur events in the larger cities. This is because a bigger proportion of the more 'cultured' citizens devote time to them. But in any art the best amateur work is less distinguished than is to be seen at the best professional shows in the larger cities. It must be so. And let us agree that gazing at stars is a very real consolation if you are not allowed to fly or even jump. But surely it is in a society where the sports, the arts, the crafts, and the exercises of the mind are most widely diffused and practised, that you have the most valuable culture.

An immensely important thing about voluntary or amateur cultural activity is that it throws people together, reveals qualities below the mannered surface, and leads naturally to personal friendships and wide acquaintanceships. Many of these activities cut across the tendency to group by income, education, and religious or political affiliations; this is particularly noticeable in some of the dramatic societies, the sports clubs (especially cricket clubs), and the scientific, health, and public welfare organizations. People drop into each other's houses to discuss and prepare for all sorts of events, and thereby get to know each other's families in a natural and informal way. These are the things that make and bind a 'community'. The same people might go for years to professional theatres, concerts, music halls, lectures, football matches, and sit side by side, without getting to know each other at all; even if they reached the stage of polite recognition of often-seen faces there would be no real appreciation of personality. To know people you must do things together with them, see them excited, making effort, off their guard, in states of enthusiasm or annoyance. When they become real in this way, you are drawn to some and repelled from others; a complex of regard, of dislike, of admiration, of criticism, even of love and hatred, grows up. And whenever, as a citizen of a smallish town, you walk along its streets, or sit in its restaurants or public-houses, or attend any kind of performance or function in it, you will encounter many people who are not merely faces to you, but persons. Almost certainly you will exchange a few words with some of them on matters of common interest. If you go to a theatre or concert, or have a meal in a restaurant, in a very big city, you are among a sea of unknown faces, and if you happen upon anyone you know it is like the meeting of Stanley and

Livingstone in Darkest Africa. I know there are people who prefer the isolation and anonymity of vast crowds. *Chacun à son gout;* but there can be no doubt as to which is Civilization, which is Society.

In any good amateur culture distinguished performers will now and then appear, and the garden cities have contributed at least their rateable percentage to professional art. From a milieu of merely receptive theatregoers, balletomanes, gallery-trampers, and lecture-eaters, drifting around from one well publicized show to another, creative artists are less likely to spring; moreover, the commercialization of the arts these wandering souls depend on tends to divorce the artists from the life of which their art must be an expression if it is to have significance at all. To me it is a miracle that in the highly organized amusement centres a genuinely creative and human piece of work so often gets through and survives. It is far from my purpose, however, to depreciate metropolitan art, or to deny that the flowers of small town culture, including that of the garden cities, are seldom exhibition blooms of the size and quality to be found in the big centres. My point is that, metaphorically as well as literally, a town of many gardens is healthier, and gives not less aesthetic joy to its inhabitants, than a town of backyards with some tropical glass-houses in its market-place. It would be nice if all towns could have the glass-houses as well as the gardens. If we cannot have both, it is not the gardens that I would do without.

Of course many garden city people succeed in making the best of both these worlds, taking part in local culture and keeping touch also with professional art and entertainment. The latter they can do in two ways: by occasional expeditions to London and other towns, and by inviting distinguished artists to their own towns. Not being compelled to spend hours per day in suburban trains, they find an occasional jaunt to another centre a pleasure; and in peace-time the L.N.E.R., by special fares and fast theatre trains out and back, have facilitated such expeditions and have found they provide a useful 'off-peak' load. In the case of the more highly-organized entertainments—opera, symphony orchestras and musical comedy, for instance—this is likely to prove the permanent means of contact. But in the case of solo musicians, eminent lecturers, string quartets and concert parties, or other artists working singly or in small groups, it is obviously more economical for artists to travel to their audiences than for hundreds of people to travel to the artists. At Welwyn this possibility has been realized; one of the local music clubs, for example, has found it possible to engage soloists and string quartets of international rank, and to pay adequate fees to the artists, at less cost to the members than the usual admission prices to concerts of the same artists in London—apart from the saving of time and fares. It only needs a club of 250 to 300 members to make this sort of arrangement practicable; and it is likely that both towns will develop it further in a number of fields of culture, including sport and light entertainment.

It is true in the garden cities, as it is in all British towns, that for a great many people group activity of any kind forms a small part of life. This is a matter often overlooked: the extent to which the masses, even in big cities, 'keep themselves to themselves', confine their interests to their homes and a few personal and family friends, and are independent of external culture or entertainment. To the poster-conscious, London seems a city of millions of people sharing in the higher forms of art; but in reality those who keep in touch with art movements, who attend orchestral concerts and the opera, even who go regularly to theatres, are a small minority. There are far larger numbers for whom the whole of culture outside their homes is summed up in the cinema, and the whole of community life in the fraternization of the public-house or registered club. Ardent minorities attend football or cricket matches, race meetings and dog tracks; and still smaller groups are active in church circles and political movements. This is not to say that the majority are cut off from the ideas or culture of the national society; but apart from the cinema their contact is through newspapers, books and verbal report, and nowadays by the immensely important medium of radio; all of which are as available in a small town as in a large one.*

Thus for the great majority of people, even of those coming straight from big cities, life in a garden city is more, not less, communal and varied. They can continue the cinema-going habit, though they like a choice of several cinemas, and it is a fair complaint of Welwyn that only one is available. (A second was about to be built when the war stopped development.) If they are actively political or religious, they can and do almost invariably join the church or party group to which they have been attached, and these are the quickest ways for newcomers to link on to community life, if they do not readily find friends at their workplaces. Both towns were, in peacetime, organized to welcome and incorporate new residents and to introduce them to circles of common interest. It is not at all difficult for those who want to take part in community life to do so. At the same time those who prefer an entirely private life can follow their bent without interference. The people of the towns are numerous enough, and themselves busy enough, not to be particularly concerned about the chosen way of life of any individual or family.

It is not possible, however, to live an 'anonymous' political or community life. That is to say, you cannot throw your weight about at meetings or in pressure groups, and at the same time conceal such activities from your workmates, your neighbours, or your employers. If you speak on public affairs at meetings, or take part in committees for any kind of movement or propaganda, you become a public figure, and the line you take will be discussed by the community in the light of all that is known about your personality. In a big amorphous city it is possible to be a revolutionary agitator or a defier of convention in your spare time, and a docile employee and conformist in your work time. And when people have been accustomed to this dualism in their lives the necessity of choosing to be one or the other all the time may come as a severe test. It even appears as a loss of freedom. In reality it is of course an accession of freedom—the addition of freedom's positive to its negative side.

If a man wants to nurse a private unconventionality, wherever he may live, he can do it in his own home or in his thoughts. If he becomes a missionary for his ideals he must want to be an effective missionary—not a voice shouting to a shifting crowd in Hyde Park who haven't the least idea who he is or whether he really means it. It is true that in a small town he will be held responsible for what he says. That is because he counts as a personality, whereas in Hyde Park he can be ignored as a nonentity. It is true also that in a small town there could be, and sometimes is, a tyrannical suppression of minority opinion; dominant personalities in some towns do in fact make it impracticable for certain views to be expressed, and even for people to live their private lives in any unorthodox way. Tyranny of that kind does not in fact exist in Letchworth and Welwyn. Except in regard to sheer criminality or habits threatening to the innocent, the degree of toleration is high. Busybodies disposed to censor other people's ideas or way of life receive no general support. It is extremely important for the future of small towns that a tolerant social atmosphere shall prevail; and some small towns have yet to appreciate this truth. Even spiteful gossip can limit the self-expression of the sensitive, and is therefore a social nuisance. But comparing notes about known persons need not be spiteful, even if it is correctly labelled as gossip. In that sense being talked about is the inevitable corollary of being a personality. I think the garden cities have reached a very sound balance in this matter; interest has not been perverted to intolerance.

Another test that I think the garden cities pass is that of a reasonable balance between attachment to their own affairs and awareness of the larger world outside. They are reasonably free both of what metropolitans call 'provincialism' and of what the Germans used to call 'Kleinstädterei' (small-townishness). It may be that everywhere these phenomena are passing; that the radio and the spread of reading may be in course of making the whole world cosmopolitan, and even weakening the local variations of culture which are the good side of 'provincialism'. There is always a tendency for any strong and self-reliant culture to be unaware of its 'municipal limits': Emerson, not without justification, made that criticism even of Londoners of such world-wide fame as Hogarth, Thackeray, Macaulay, and Hallam, and his accusation that Dickens wrote 'London Tracts' is not to be dismissed as a mere reprisal for *American Notes*. It can still be said that, in Emerson's sense, the most 'provincial' city in England is London; because it does contain large numbers of people so centred on the peculiar culture of its West End, or of narrow coteries therein, that they do not know of the existence of high cultures of a different flavour in other parts of England; whereas even in the most self-centred of other regions it is at least known that London exists. The situation of Letchworth and Welwyn within easy reach of London and Cambridge would not in any case have permitted of the development of provincialism or 'Kleinstädterei' in an extreme degree. But apart from that, I do not think under present conditions any towns based on modern industry would tend to these social vices.

Of the two garden cities, Letchworth is more self-centred, more 'provincial' in this unabusive sense, than Welwyn. I do not cite this as either a merit or a defect; merely as a fact. No one would wish that all towns should be the same. Each of the garden cities has an atmosphere of its own. I do not feel called upon to define in any detail their special qualities; and it would embarrass me to do so, since I am a resident of one and an ex-resident of the other and each is very properly convinced of certain superiorities, not only to other towns, but particularly to the other garden city. The dates of foundation of the two towns have influenced their respective characters; and still more these have been shaped by the personalities of their promoting groups and early residents.

The note of Letchworth, perhaps, in its early days, was that of search for a new and more brotherly way of life; bound up with this was its character of social informality (which it retains) and of revolt against the conventionality of the time when it was started; the town had a name once for unorthodoxy, in dress, in political ideas, in religion. But in this it expressed in its own way the social ideas of the advanced spirits of the early years of this century; as in housing, so in personal habits and popular thought, Letchworth was among the leaders. If it has lost its lead, it is because the world has caught up with its special originality, and it has not yet thought of anything to be newly original about.

The early note of Welwyn was less rebellious and more stylish; in architecture, in dress, in social ways, it rather expressed the latest development of accepted thought than sought a turn in a new and different direction. It is now perhaps more alert to the emergence of new ideas in the world at large than Letchworth is. Whether that is a merit or not must depend on personal judgment. The final term of complete world-awareness is cosmopolitanism, and I cannot think that that is desirable. But these differences between the two towns are after all marginal. I rejoice that at heart both remain English in prevailing character; that they are small enough, and are intended always to be small enough, for personalities and particular interests to influence their character; and that their social and community life is additional to and does not replace their family life. Where homes are good and family life is strong, society is in no danger of being standardized.

I have given some idea of the vigour of voluntary or amateur culture in the two towns. In both, however, I am sure, there are many residents who are not entirely satisfied with this. I do not think this is due to a craving for higher cultural standards; it is more likely that these people have insufficient social energy left over from their daily work; they wish to be amused without too much effort. They would like a wider choice and a more regular provision of professional entertainment. It is the aim of the estate managements to do more than has yet been done to cater for this demand, and much discussion goes on as to what are the most important next steps. Welwyn, as I have said, has only one cinema; Letchworth has two. These, in their choice of films, naturally make their appeal to the greatest common denominator of the public; they do not meet the more selective demand—a deprivation to the minority who are bored (as I confess I often am) by the average film. Towns of this social composition really need three cinemas each; two of moderate size under competing managements, and a smaller one for special films, including amateur films. Neither town yet possesses a first-class theatre building at which plays can be regularly given—perhaps by a repertory company alternating with amateur groups—nor a specially designed concert hall. The Welwyn theatre (seating 1,100) is an excellent building for stage plays, but, except for the annual Drama Festival Week and an occasional musical play by a local society, it is given over to films. The Barn theatre seats only 120—too small for sound economics even in the case of amateur societies, and impossibly small for visits by professional repertory companies. There are in both towns other halls in which dramatic performances are given, but the full development of good drama requires really well-designed theatres of an appropriate size. Letchworth has a presentable library building and local museum; Welwyn is still carrying on its library (surprisingly well considering the disadvantages) in a former dwelling house. Neither town has yet a suitable place in which painting and sculpture can be shown, though temporary exhibitions are held occasionally in public halls. There are other shortages, but these are the most felt.

Making them good is only partly a matter of population. Even now the towns could support on a remunerative basis the institutions I have named. After the war they are certain to do so as soon as building permits can be obtained. In my view it would have been worth while, had the capital position permitted, to provide a theatre and concert hall in advance of the economic demand. Buildings of the right sort are not cheap, but their cost is small in relation to the total cost of a town. If you are building say 5,000 houses at a cost (pre-war) of two million pounds, an allocation of £5 or £10 per house (£25,000 to £50,000) would provide reasonably, if not handsomely, for cultural institutions of this type; and at least a small return on the capital could be anticipated. Their effect on the tone and prestige of a new town, and therefore on its attractiveness to modern industrialists, their workers and other residents, would be, I believe, considerable. By the time a town reaches 20,000 or 25,000, almost every essential amenity would become self-supporting. It would have helped Letchworth and Welwyn if resources had been available for such buildings at a somewhat earlier stage. And I do not think it would have checked appreciably their voluntary cultural activity.

PART THREE

GREEN-BELT CITIES: THE FUTURE

   ... When we mean to build,
We first survey the plot, then draw the model;
And when we see the figure of the house,
Then must we rate the cost of the erection. . . .
Which if we find outweighs ability,
What do we do but draw anew the model
In fewer offices, or at least desist
To build at all? Much more, in this great work,
Which is almost to pluck a kingdom down
And set another up, should we survey
The plot of situation and the model,
Consent upon a sure foundation,
Question surveyors, know our own estate,
How able such a work to undergo.
        Shakespeare: *Henry IV*, Part II, Act I (3)

The Lord Bardolph was not of the breed that rebuilds kingdoms, but in this speech he certainly put the stages of the process in right sequence. Desire and will first; then provisional design; and then the survey of site and resources to find out how what is intended can be done. To-day there are many people, thinking themselves 'scientific', who would reverse this order and try to derive what ought to be from a study of what is. Piling around themselves mountains of research material, they become so impressed by the refinements of economic and social interaction that have led to the existing arrangement of cities that it begins to seem an impiety to cut across that exquisite complex of cause and effect by the exercise of crude human will. 'Whoever discredits analogy', said Emerson, 'and requires heaps of facts, before any theories can be attempted, has no poetic power, and nothing original or beautiful will ever be produced by him.'[1] At first I

[1] *English Traits:* essay on *Literature*.

129

thought him unjust to the English when he added that as a nation we lack the faculty of generalization:

'The absence of the faculty in England is shown by the timidity which accumulates mountains of facts, as a bad general wants myriads of men and miles of redoubts, to compensate the inspirations of courage and conduct.'[1] But when I think of the mass of investigations and reports that have gathered around the subject of planning in the last few years, and of the absence of constructive action in this field, I begin to see more truth in Emerson's criticism than I like. Yet if he were here to examine the truck-loads of admirable surveys that have descended on me from America in the same years, he might suspect that the lack is not peculiarly English. In the sphere of town development the Lord-Bardolphian strain in our minds is in a phase of dominance; the Platonic and Baconian strain is in a phase of recession. Somehow we must recover the power to generate ideals and to come to decisions.*

We shall never rebuild our towns to suit ourselves unless we set out with an idea, or concept, of the sort of towns we want. I showed in my second chapter how such a concept is beginning to emerge from the fusing of many sectional desires. The prescience of Howard has helped to formulate that concept, and, more important, has provided us with a design that is in large measure satisfying. And while other thinkers and writers on planning have been groping their way towards the principles of that same design, the two models described in this book have been built to illustrate and to test it. I come now to consider some of the practical lessons to be learned from these experimental towns, and to suggest the measures required to apply their experience and to improve upon their achievements.

[1] Ibid.

Chapter VII

A NATIONAL POLICY OF DISPERSAL

The Meaning of Dispersal

Between 1941 and 1945 the Government accepted, by cautious stages, the principles of urban development recommended by the Barlow Royal Commission, thus expressed in the Commission's Report:[1]

'(a) Continued and further redevelopment of congested urban areas, where necessary.

'(b) Decentralization or dispersal, both of industries and industrial population, from such areas.

'(c) Encouragement of a reasonable balance of industrial development, as far as possible, throughout the various divisions or regions of Great Britain, coupled with appropriate diversification of industry in each division or region throughout the country.'

The Barlow Report had also proposed a 'Central Planning Authority' to formulate the policy or plan for decentralization or dispersal, and to work out, for the different areas, how population and industry should be regrouped—in garden cities, garden suburbs, satellite towns, trading estates, or extensions of existing small towns or regional centres. In 1941 the Government accepted this proposal for a Central Planning Authority; and in 1943 the new Ministry of Town and Country Planning was set up. And in 1944 the Government accepted in principle the 'main ideas' of the Barlow Report: the 'decongestion of congested areas' and 'the spreading out of those congested areas over wider areas'.[2]*

To me the language used in these official statements seemed needlessly heavy and wary. 'Decentralization' and 'decongestion' might have meant several different things: (a) a transfer of part of a central population to suburbs, leaving industry in the centre,

---

[1] *Report of the Royal Commission on the Distribution of the Industrial Population* (H.M.S.O., 1940).

[2] Rt. Hon. Hugh Dalton, M.P., President of the Board of Trade, in House of Commons, 7th June 1944.

which was of course the type of development that prevailed in the inter-war period; (b) a movement of both industry and workers to industrial suburbs of the unorganized type of Edgware (London), or of the organized type of Wythenshawe (Manchester) or Speke (Liverpool); or (c) a regrouping of industry and people, from overcrowded centres, in new towns or country towns some distance away.

For some time there was doubt as to which of these methods the Government preferred. But the important Town and Country Planning Act of 1944, and certain other specific and incidental statements, made it apparent that it was the third method that the Government had primarily in mind. The main purpose of this Act is to endow local planning authorities with new powers to acquire land for planning and redevelopment; and among these are powers to acquire land for 'providing for re-location of population or industry'. By Section 1 (2) and 9 (2) 're-location' is defined, in relation to war-damaged areas or areas of obsolete layout, as:

'Rendering available elsewhere than in that area, whether in an existing community or in a community to be newly established, accommodation for residential purposes or for the carrying on of business or other activities, together with all other appropriate public services, facilities for public worship, recreation and amenity, and other requirements, being accommodation to be rendered available for persons or undertakings who are living or carrying on business or other activities in that area or who were doing so but by reason of war circumstances are no longer for the time being doing so, and whose continued or resumed location in that area would be inconsistent with the proper planning thereof.'

Here the pattern is clear. And the term that has now been generally accepted for re-location of people and businesses in smaller communities is 'dispersal'. Note that this word 'dispersal', as now used in connection with town and country planning, does not mean scattering of population and industry at large in the countryside. For that process, which no planner wants, the appropriate label is 'diffusion'. The term 'dispersal' has come to mean the transfer of the excess of industry, business and people from overcrowded centres to new towns or rural sites, and to existing country towns which can be extended without producing new congestion or overgrowth.*

These reception centres, whether new towns or extended country towns, must not be sited right on the fringes of great urban masses; otherwise we shall only be rationalizing the process of suburban growth. They must be separated from the parent cities, and from other towns, by wide stretches of permanently reserved farm land. The pattern to aim at is that of towns of moderate size, complete communities in which people both live and work, on a background of green country. It is the 'garden city' pattern as Howard meant it, and as I have defined it in this book.

Scale and Pace of Dispersal

How much dispersal from congested cities is needed to bring their density down to a point at which their remaining citizens can find the right amount of space for their life and work? The answer must depend on the standard of density to be adopted in central rebuilding; and also (since in rebuilding we are dealing with a long-lasting fabric) on our views as to the future size of our population.*

In making my estimates of the required amount of dispersal I do not feel it right to assume a permanent decline in the population. It is true that in the years just before the 1939–45 War the reproduction rate in Great Britain was about 0·8—that is to say, the babies born were only four-fifths of the number necessary to maintain the population. The continuing small increase in the total population was due to the lengthening of the average life: we were becoming an older population; and if the established trend continued, within a decade or so our total numbers would cease to grow. The number of families was still increasing, but this curve was nearing its top, and before many years an actual decline of the number of families seemed almost certain to set in.

During the war there has been (not only in Great Britain but in most industrial countries) a remarkable increase in the birth-rate; but this does not necessarily mean that the trend has changed, or that the threatened decline of population has been avoided. It may mean only that war has advanced the date of some marriages and the birth of first babies of these marriages; we cannot say that the reproduction rate is recovering until we know that the average pair of parents is producing a larger family, and of that there is as yet no evidence.

Nevertheless in considering long-term planning policy I disregard the prospect of a positive fall in population: for two reasons. First, our own nation is roused as to the possibility, and regards it as a danger; social policy is certain to do anything that can be done to avoid it, and personal policy is likely to be responsive to the strong national sentiment gathering around the subject. Second, planning policy, in my opinion, is itself a factor of prime importance in the restoration of the birth-rate.

The connection is subtle, and it would take me too far from the subject of this book to discuss it fully. Cause and effect in this field are not easy to distinguish. But I am sure there is the closest possible relationship between the way of life in family homes with gardens and a reasonable standard of space and privacy, the strength of family idealism, and the reproduction rate. To take the simplest instance: where family idealism is in retreat more people will be disposed to cut down their home accommodation to the service-flat standard, more married women will centre their interests on work careers rather than on the home, more time will be spent by husbands and wives on activities outside the dwelling and less within it, and babies will be fewer. Stockholm and Vienna, the classic cities of the flat, are also the cities of the lowest birth-rates. But whether people choose to live in flats because the accent of their lives is outside the family, or whether that accent arises from the necessity of living in flats or apartment houses, can be argued about indefinitely.

As a housing manager I observed the way of life of many households for many years. My judgment is that the action is reciprocal; each of these phenomena flows from and produces the other. People of the non-family type, more interested in professional work or external cultural pursuits than in the home and children, prefer dwellings of the service-flat type because they want the maximum leisure and energy for their real interests. But I have seen many cases where the necessity of starting married life in rooms or a flat, against a young couple's true inclinations, has caused a postponement of the family; both partners have continued at work; and the double income and freedom from household responsibilities have set up a pattern of life, with advantages of its own, which has become habitual and has smothered the initial impulse to found a family—an enterprise requiring a great deal of courage if undertaken in cold blood.

Thus it seems to me to make no difference, in practical politics, at which point we choose to break in on this circle. Whether the national resolve to restore the birth-rate will cause us to do all we can to build houses of the type family-minded people want, or whether a revival of family idealism and a desire to have more children will increase the effective demand for family homes, the outcome is the same. In either case national policy will have to provide the maximum number of houses suited in size and character to be family homes. I start from this. I see little practical value for housing policy in demographic statistics which prove that there are a great many two-person households for whom in theory a two-roomed or three-roomed dwelling could be made to do. The two-person family at any one moment of time is the four-person to six-person family of to-morrow or yesterday; and people do not want to move house whenever a baby is born or a young person leaves the nest, though that detestable practice is thrust on tenants of council houses in some congested cities. Families will at times exercise their own freedom to move; and many do so when the breadwinner gets a new job or economic circumstances change. But young couples usually prefer to start life in a house suited to a future family; and often an old couple wishes to stay on in the family home when the children have grown up and left it. Housing policy should foster, not thwart, this desire for the continuity of the home. It follows that the great majority of houses should be houses in which a normal family, at its numerical peak, can be comfortable. It is all to the good if at other times in the family history there are spare rooms and spare space.

The analogy of the legislation relating to minimum standards of wages, before family allowances were enacted, may be cited. In order to discover what would be minimum income for subsistence it was necessary to assume that the family to be supported was a family that would ensure the continuance of the race, and in the studies of the subject (for example by Mr. Seebohm Rowntree) it was customary to take as a datum the family of man, wife, and three children. Clearly it is important to take no lower datum

when considering the types of dwelling house that are to be predominant in our housing schemes. Houses are built to last for at
least sixty years; the loans are arranged to be paid off over that
period; and in fact the houses may, if well built, last much longer.
The layout of streets and services proves in practice more permanent still. Not only is it financially improvident to build houses
and to rebuild towns without forethought for the likely or possible
composition of families for three or four generations ahead; it is,
from a national point of view, suicidal to build and plan deliberately for a disappearing population.

Again, in this question of the scale of dispersal, I think we are
bound to assume a rising rather than a static or declining standard
of the real income of the majority of people. We may not entirely
achieve the national aim of full employment; but that an approach
to it is practicable is now economic orthodoxy; and any advance
in that direction means a spread of prosperity downward through
the various levels of income. This, among other things, will produce
a rise in the standard of housing demanded by the mass of people.

Recent experience shows clearly what this implies as to the form
of urban development. In the period from 1901 to 1938, when real
incomes were rising substantially in south-east England, well over
$1\frac{1}{2}$ million people moved out of the congested County of London,
mostly to the suburbs.[1] Natural increase (excess of births over
deaths) masked the movement to some extent, but even the net
decline in the County amounted to 450,000. It is well known that
it was mainly the more prosperous elements of the population
that went out. This outward tendency went on right up to the
war. It cannot be arrested by a policy of flat building, because
nine out of ten families, with every opportunity of making fair
comparisons, strongly prefer single family houses with gardens.

The demand for houses with gardens could be met, in any large
city, by a continuance of the building of suburbs coupled with the
extension of transport services. And in the absence of proper planning, that is the way in which it would in fact be met. In practice,
therefore, the choice is not between high-density redevelopment
and some form of decentralization. High-density development on
a large scale is simply not practical politics if people are left with

---

[1] This was the outward migration *on balance;* the number of individuals who
actually moved out was of course vastly greater.

any degree of free choice as to where they will live. The real choice is between two alternatives only: that of a further huge exodus to suburbs (followed or accompanied by sporadic outward movements of industries and offices, also to the suburbs, leaving big derelict areas in the centres); and that of an intelligent dispersal to new and existing country towns.

The measure of the dispersal to be planned for therefore depends on judgment as to the standard of density which will permit of acceptable living conditions in the areas now congested. I have mentioned in Chapter II the official estimates of the displacement of population necessary from London and certain other cities. In the L.C.C. Plan (1943) the final dispersal from the County of London was estimated at roundly 600,000, bringing the County population down to about 3,330,000. The central areas to be first redeveloped, for a future population of nearly 2,000,000, were mainly to have maximum densities of 200 and 136 persons per acre, and four acres of open space per 1,000; and the latest official estimate (given in the *Greater London Plan* 1944) is that this would mean that of these two million central Londoners 70 per cent would have to live in flats. To my mind this is a totally impossible project. Making all allowances for the selective accumulation, in the centre of a metropolis of 8½ millions, of the 'non-family' elements of society, there cannot be enough of these in a self-reproducing population to carry that number of flats. Even if we were to accept central London as a racial erosion area—a luxury the nation cannot afford—it is unlikely that we shall long continue to recruit sufficient volunteers to keep it occupied on that vast scale. The evidence of popular opinion in the eastern boroughs of London makes it clear that to hold a normal population permanently a much higher proportion of single-family dwellings will have to be provided on redevelopment.

The official estimates for other cities are nearer the mark, but still, viewed realistically, on the low side. But even these, with the London official estimates, imply a displacement of two million people from half a dozen big cities only. If we maintain or slightly increase our total population in the next twenty-five to fifty years, I do not think my round estimate that four to five million people will have to be provided for in new towns and town extensions is far wrong.

As to the pace of this process of dispersal, it will be governed by the pace of the national rebuilding effort. From the planning point of view this is a secondary issue. Whether we rebuild rapidly or slowly, the desirable pattern of relocation is the same. The Government programme is to build about four million houses in the first ten or twelve years after the war, and to achieve this programme along with repair work and other kinds of building in proportion it is intended to increase the number of building operatives, who were just over a million in 1939, to a million and a quarter by about 1949. This means training a large number of skilled trades-men, and the expanded force could, in twenty years from 1945, easily build eight million houses and other classes of buildings in normal ratio thereto. Some economists think this would be to devote too large a share of our resources in manpower and materials to the single purpose of building. They would reduce the quantum of building and apply more of our productive power to industrial re-equipment, defence, and goods for export. The matter deserves careful thought, because there must be a proper balance between the competing claims on manpower and mater-ials. I would argue for high priority for the building and rebuilding of houses, factories and community equipment; and I think a successful full employment policy would enable this to be under-taken without any lessening of the manpower allocated to the other important purposes.

It would be a sound social investment for Great Britain, besides repairing bomb damage and overtaking the present housing shor-tage, to replace the greater part of its pre-1914 dwellings in twenty to twenty-five years. Ninety per cent of the $8\frac{1}{2}$ million pre-1914 dwellings in our towns and villages are out of date by present standards. By 1970 none of them would be less than sixty years old. I do not overlook that there are many fine ancient buildings that ought to be religiously preserved, and that some part of the programme should take the form of the reconditioning and adaptation to changed requirements of any buildings which are essentially satisfactory in fabric and of distinguished design. But in the vast areas of uninteresting and substandard dwellings in our towns and cities, these good old houses are a small percentage. Moreover, proper reconditioning and adaptation, to make the accommodation entirely satisfactory, though it may be more economical than rebuilding in some cases, is not so much more economical, and does not extend to a sufficient number of houses, to affect appreciably the scale of the operation. We are faced with a programme equivalent in any case to the replacement of something like eight million houses.

The programme that is desirable when you look at the condition of our stock of buildings thus coincides very closely with the capacity of the expanded building industry: the equivalent of eight million houses in twenty years, together with other classes of buildings in like proportion. Our planning policy should seek to place all these buildings rightly. It is not necessary nor advisable to be dogmatic about the period. That can be regarded as adjustable in the light of economic conditions. The number may also have to be adjusted if there is a marked change in the reproduction rate. The broad picture however is this. In a period of not less than twenty years, and almost certainly not more than thirty years, we shall be rehousing, and providing improved workplaces and community buildings for, something like twenty-eight million people. Of these it is probable that about twenty-three millions can be provided for by the more open rebuilding of existing built-up areas. It is only for the balance of about five millions that new towns and extensions of country towns will be needed. That is a small part of the total programme. But it is essential to the proper conduct of the larger operation, and it is quite a substantial operation in itself.

Though the time over which the whole rebuilding programme is spread may be elastic, there is no similar elasticity about the time within which decisions affecting its character and pattern should be made. The war has created opportunities which can be lost by making a start in the wrong way. There has been a great deal of displacement of persons and industry, through evacuation, strategic dispersal, and bomb damage. (The population of the County of London, for instance, was reduced during the war from four millions to two and a half millions.) In some congested cities, notably in London, a number of factory and office buildings have been destroyed, and the businesses therein discontinued or transferred elsewhere. Some of the displaced businesses will want to return to their former situations; some indeed must do so by reason of their essentially local character. But many desire to stay out, and many are undecided but would be willing to settle permanently in smaller towns if provision can be quickly made for suitable buildings.

Evacuation, military service, and vast transfers of workers to wartime occupations, have also (tragically enough) cut or loosened many local ties which cannot be or need not be rejoined. The upheaval of war and the pause in building have made a rearrangement of homes, workplaces and communities much less difficult than it would be in ordinary times when the interlocking machine of urban development is at full speed. We have a unique chance of restarting in a new direction if we can see how to take it.

Chapter VIII

WAYS AND MEANS OF DISPERSAL

The Siting of New Towns

There is a vast literature on the historical causes for the position and growth of existing towns. Into these causes have entered many accidents and many arbitrary human choices. Most writers seem to me to assume too easily that what has happened must have been for the best. But some successful towns are poorly sited, and many could have been on a number of alternative sites and still have flourished. Even where a town has grown up 'naturally' the reason for its exact position may often be found, not in the total economic, political or social merits of the site, but in some past convenience for one or two influential persons pursuing a narrow interest. Often an uncertain balance of advantage between many possible situations must have been tipped to this side or that by the chance that some early building was occupied by a man of energy, business talent, or military power. A small minority of the world's towns were sited by deliberate choice, and even when this happened the data for the choice were pretty sketchy. What I think the record shows is how much latitude there is in the siting of towns from the economic, military, political or architectural points of view that have usually been dominant, and the general absence of concern for permanently good living conditions for the largest classes of citizens.

One has only to read of the schoolboyish proposal made to Alexander of Macedon by Dinocrates for a new city on Mount Athos,[1] and to recall that after that display of ineptitude the great king still made Dinocrates his pet new-town architect, to suspect that the siting of the Greco-Macedonian colonial cities was none too clever. I am not sure that the method previously used by Ilos

---

[1] His brainwave was that the mountain should be carved into the form of a human statue, holding the new town in one hand and an ornamental lake in the other. Alexander turned it down on the ground that there was no agricultural land nearby for the citizens' food supply.

in founding Troy—following a spotted cow around until it settled with a contented moo in the water-meadows under the forest-screened slopes of Mount Ida—was not as good as most. It is more pleasing than the commoner classical method of studying the entrails of sacrificed animals. I am conscious that the spotted cow defied the Scott Report principle of keeping new towns off the best grassland, to which I refer later; but in this she was true to one of the few historical generalizations that can be made about town siting. Towns usually sprang up where the agricultural population was most dense, and that was naturally on the most fruitful land. London is a case in point. No one would question the unique merits of the situation of London; yet if that city were being started to-day its naked site would pass few of the tests which planners using the geographical 'sieve' would apply. Not only was the land highly productive, but much of the site was liable to flooding; the aesthetic filter would have ruled out much of the site as far too attractive for urban masses to live upon; and the superb land communications that now make London the nodal point of England are much more the result than the cause of the city's being where it is. The River Thames was London's trump card; most of its other enormous technical advantages have been added by human labour.

I indulge in this historical excursus, not to extol chance at the expense of forethought, but to bring out the point that, in town siting as in other matters, the will (even the caprice) of man is the master of circumstance. Past town siting has reflected past balances of social and economic power, besides depending on many irrational accidents. The balance of power is shifting. At one time a margin of a fractional percentage in factory costs, or the passion of a managing director's wife to live in a metropolis, or the desire of a business executive to hunt, shoot and play golf, were decisive factors in the location of factories employing thousands of people, and therefore of the situation and growth of towns. To-day the interests of those thousands begins to throw more weight in the balance. They will even affect the economic calculation when the cost of journeys to work is brought into the account. The state of existing communications may be less important in the choice than the pleasantness of the site as a home for a future community. Man can still make roads—and even railways. Too often the subject is discussed as if we must accept the existing framework of communications as a geographical limiting factor. That would be so for a small builder deciding where to build a dozen villas. It is not so when a great industrial nation is considering the best layout of its towns and countryside as a whole.

Who is to choose the sites for new towns? The matter is so important to a nation that there ought to be powers of initiative and guidance, and powers of veto, in the hands of a central state department (in Great Britain the Ministry of Town and Country Planning) capable of some balancing from the national point of view of the complex of social, economic, strategic and aesthetic considerations involved. But entire centralization of initiative is neither practicable nor desirable. No central mind or group of minds can comprehend the immense range of existing and emerging factors or replace the widespread driving forces that create urban development. Central and regional planning control must check and canalize these forces, because if left to themselves they produce results injurious to common welfare; and where a local or private agency for a desirable new development is missing, the state should step in and fill the gap. But it may be expected that in general the choice of sites for new towns will arise from regional, local or private propositions, and that such propositions will be sifted by the regional planning mechanism in conformity with the broad national policy. Already many possible sites have been indicated in advisory regional plans. Sir Patrick Abercrombie has for example suggested ten sites for satellite towns in his *Greater London Plan* 1944. Other planning reports, and the reports of voluntary research groups, have made suggestions for various regions. Not all these reports are above criticism, either as to the sites they suggest or the sites they exclude, but they are building up a fund of proposals from which a choice can be made.

The choice, very fortunately, has not to be based on a theoretical study of what would be the ideal layout of modern industrial Great Britain if the island and its resources were a clear field for new settlement. The practical question is far simpler. It is necessary to start from things as they are, and the major drawbacks of which we are conscious. We must consider the cities to be decongested; the distances to which dispersing industries can move, having regard to their linkages with other industries; the need of rural areas for an influx of population; the existence of, or possibility of providing, basic services; and above all the suitability or adaptability of possible sites as homes for future communities. Existing communications must be studied too, though the scale of the operations in prospect may well justify new roads and in some cases new railway branches, stations and goods depots. Prospective developments whose situation will be governed by geographical factors—as for example those related to new mining areas, forestry and soil improvement schemes, factories permanently dispersed for military reasons, and air ports—must also be taken into account. But the relative importance of existing buildings or other factors may well be much less when it is definitely intended to create a town of 30,000 to 50,000, than it would be if only small piecemeal developments were envisaged.

Almost any practicable site in Great Britain, particularly if it is within striking distance of a large agglomeration and is intended as a receiving centre for that area, will include a village or two, or may even have some beginnings of development of the urban type. It is a matter for judgment in each case whether some such existing development shall be treated as the central nucleus for the new town. There were two small villages on the Letchworth estate, and parts of three on the Welwyn estate, each with its church, public-house and village shop; but none of these, for topographical reasons, was selected as a main centre; they remain small subnuclei towards the edges of the new towns. The fewer the old buildings there are on an estate, the freer the planning will be, and the less the economic structure of the new community will be troubled by vested interests. But on the other hand, skilful planning sometimes catches useful suggestions from the existing works of man, as well as from natural features. Character in towns, as in persons, as often arises from limitations as from endowments. But if there is a great deal of bad development on the site, it may not be possible to retrieve it unless extensive demolitions are undertaken.

Estates to be acquired for development should be of adequate size. A town which is designed for modern industry, employing people living on the spot, ought I think to aim at a population of at least 30,000. But in Great Britain, where we have many very large towns already, I see no present virtue in building further towns in excess of 50,000. Within these two limits a reasonable balance between physical extent and economic and social diversity can be attained; but if you go above 50,000 some of the distances between home and work, home and town centre, and home and countryside, become too great, unless you build at too high a density. The experience of Letchworth and Welwyn shows that when you have provided the space needed for advanced industries, for the true housing demands of an average population, for shops and public buildings and open-air recreation, the overall density of the town area will not exceed fourteen or fifteen persons per acre. For the town area alone therefore, the land needed, if the population aimed at is 30,000, is at least 2,000 acres; if 40,000, 2,666 acres; and if 50,000, 3,333 acres. At 15 persons per acre a town of 50,000 would have an average diameter of $2\frac{1}{2}$ miles.*

It is, I think, desirable that some part of the designated country belt of a new town shall be in the same ownership as the area intended to be built up. This makes it possible to plan together the town area and the farmland most closely related to it; it facilitates the best siting of the larger open spaces such as golf courses and cricket fields, which should be on the outer edge of the town; it brings under the town's estate management the land which is most important from the point of view of amenity and of 'protective' food production; and it is the surest way to prevent the exploitation of any prospective building value of the fringe land by outside interests. It may be hoped that the zoning of country belts around all towns will be achieved by statutory planning schemes; and when this comes about the necessity for the ownership of the whole belt by the body owning and developing the town estate will be less imperative. But for the reasons given, it is preferable that the land under single ownership should be at least three times the intended town area.*

It is not destructive of the self-dependence of a new town to place it fairly near an existing country town. But there should be a definite zone of permanently reserved open land separating them; and I would put the desirable minimum distance between the building limits of any two small towns at two to three miles. Between towns at these short distances—say four to six miles from centre to centre—there will be a great deal of interchange. Some people (the fewer the better, but it is neither desirable nor possible to thwart free choice) will live in one town and work in another, and there will be frequent inter-visiting for shopping and entertainment. Also certain public services, such as secondary and technical schools, can be planned for a group of two or three towns with advantage to all of them. Interchanges of that kind carry out Howard's fruitful conception of Social Cities. But for daily purposes for most people each of the towns of such a group should be independent; and this will come about if there is the suggested degree of physical separation between them.

On the other hand, from the point of view of the agricultural countryside it is desirable that the new towns should be well distributed. This is particularly so in the regions which have suffered population losses by the excessive centralization of the past. It is a grave mistake to keep new towns out of a predominantly agricultural area just because that area is supposed to be distinguished by an 'agricultural rhythm'.[1] The tendency of a purely agricultural population, remote from urban areas, is necessarily downward by reason of the mechanization and rationalization of farming. The war has accelerated the withdrawal of workers from the land and also the process of mechanization. In the United States there were four million fewer people living on farms in 1943 than in 1935. Great Britain had 1,500 farm tractors in 1917; 175,000 in 1944. No agricultural policy alone can stop the 'basic shift' of population from the rural areas which such figures imply. Public services—from educational facilities to water, electricity and gas—are held back; and the cultural and recreational amenities needed to retain the younger and brighter elements in agriculture cannot be economically provided. Even in the rich and advanced agricultural districts of Lincolnshire or East Anglia, a few new industrial towns would be immensely beneficial for these reasons. The siting of our new towns must be practicable from the point of view of urban industry, and this factor makes for grouping them as Social Cities and placing them within fairly easy reach of the bigger centres. But the true interests of the rural population make for wider dispersal. These factors must be carefully balanced in choosing the sites.*

A very proper concern for the safeguarding of agricultural land

[1] This seductive phrase, based on the assumptions which I here question, is to be found in Sir Patrick Abercrombie's *Greater London Plan* 1944.

and the preservation of the countryside against random building has stirred some people to natural alarm about the effects of a dispersal policy. But if you take my higher figure of a dispersal of five million people, and if you provide for them in new towns and country towns at an overall density of fifteen persons per town acre, which would give ample room for their homes, factories, public buildings and a generous allowance of open space, you would absorb only 333,000 acres of the 33 million acres of agricultural land and woodland in Great Britain, leaving the further 18 million acres of heath and moorland out of account. To use 1 per cent of the lowland countryside for giving decent living conditions to our urban masses is not to waste land or to spoil our beautiful island. Nor would it reduce food production; the food grown in the gardens of the new houses would exceed in value, as it would greatly exceed in freshness to the consumers, the food grown on the area formerly occupied by the proposed new communities. What agriculturists and lovers of the countryside justifiably fear is the unconsidered sprawling of building in the regions around great cities, which depreciates from their point of view far more land than it actually uses. Planned dispersal is the antithesis, and indeed the only practicable alternative, to 'sprawl'.

Everything else being equal, to choose land of the best market gardening quality (of which there is only a small acreage in Great Britain) for new urban development would be thriftless. But we ought not to go to the opposite extreme and place our new towns on the poorest soils. Some of our very best soil, in Lincolnshire and Cornwall for example, is devoted, with every economic and social justification, to the growing of cut flowers and bulbs. Hundreds of thousands of acres are used for the production of hops and barley for alcoholic beverages; and there are few to-day who would contend that this is (even in wartime) an improper diversion of land which ought to have been used for wheat and potatoes to make this country more independent in its food supply. Here again a wise balancing of all the considerations is needed; and planning will be distorted if the desire to retain every possible acre of good land for farming dominates all other desires. Town gardens and allotments, which produce for their occupiers much food, many flowers, and the most healthful of spare time pursuits, have a high claim for good land. And playing fields have a similar claim. It is only the important stretches of precious and rare market-gardening land that should be particularly avoided in the siting of towns; and if small pieces of such land occur within a town area, the plan should put them to appropriate use.

There is a further point which is often overlooked. Land in the neighbourhood of towns has in the past often been cut up into awkward pieces, and the future of much of it is uncertain. No one knows whether or when it will be built on. Hence no new agricultural capital is spent on it; even maintenance is neglected, and it deteriorates as farm land. But much land in that sort of position would be well worth cultivation at a high level if its status as farm land were permanently assured. It is the nearest land to the market, and would have higher not lower agricultural value by reason of its situation. On a planned estate it would be known what land will remain agricultural and what land will sooner or later be built on. Under these conditions land can be properly farmed right up to the very edge of a town, and untidiness and waste can be avoided.

Promotion and Finance of New Towns

If the new towns are to be put in the right places, the sites must be acquired by compulsory purchase, whoever is to develop them. The Letchworth inquiries showed that suitable estates are not at all likely to be found in the single ownership of willing sellers. Welwyn's miraculous luck is not likely to be repeated. Almost always the site will be held by a number of owners, any one of whom could kill the scheme or hold it up to ransom. Sites for garden cities can be purchased, either for a local authority or a limited-profit body, with the consent of the Ministry, under section 35 of the Town and Country Planning Act, 1932. Or for schemes related to dispersal from war-damaged or obsolete city areas, sites could be purchased under sections 1, 9 or 10 of the Town and Country Planning Act 1944. Alternatively, sites could be acquired, with the consent of the Ministry of Health, under section 73 of the Housing Act, 1936. The powers of subsequent development under each of these Acts vary. I think it is possible that in some cases the powers under the Acts of 1936 and 1944 could be used in combination. But it would be better if, in a future

Act, straightforward and inclusive powers were given for a Ministry, or a public corporation, a local authority, one or more local authorities in combination, or a limited-profit body, with the consent of a Ministry, to acquire sites for complete towns and to undertake all forms of development and building thereon. Each of the sections at present available imposes certain restrictions that would be hampering in practice. There is a useful precedent for wider developmental powers in the Liverpool Corporation Act of 1936.*

There are many different bodies that might promote and build new towns, or take some part in doing so: and I would like to see them all at work—state corporations, local authorities, urban and rural; private enterprise, including estate companies, groups of landowners, building societies, and great constructional firms; limited dividend associations and co-operative societies. The corporations of big cities might acquire the sites for their own satellite towns, undertake the estate development, construct roads and public services, build many of the houses, and provide, or lease sites for, factories, shops, and other buildings. Or sites might be owned and main development be done by local authorities of the areas in which the new towns are situated; in some cases by two or more authorities in combination. Under the Town and Country Planning Act 1944 the authority of a congested city area may enter into an agreement with one or more authorities in a rural area for the joint creation of a new town; either party handling the main development, housing, or the provision of services. In any of these cases private enterprise could take leases from the town promoting authority and play a large part in subdevelopment or building any class of properties. Or the complete town development might be undertaken by private enterprise on sites acquired by a public authority (1944 Act, section 20).*

In my opinion, Howard's method is, all things considered, the best: the ownership of the town site by a body having the freedom of action of private enterprise, with a limit on its profits. While therefore the other methods—public enterprise and private enterprise—should undoubtedly be used as well, I suggest that special attention be paid to devising agencies of the intermediate type. Having had experience in garden city administration both as estate manager of one of the companies and as clerk and finance officer of one of the local authorities, I have been able to compare the inherent merits and demerits of current forms of public enterprise and limited-profit private enterprise. A local government officer has always to be consulting statutes and orders to see what his authority can do (and often he finds it can't); he is responsible to a council elected for every sort of admirable reason except knowledge of the kind of businesses the council has to run; the council is in turn responsible to an electorate which, when it takes an active interest in anything, usually gets excited about some side issue of council business and does not see the picture as a whole; the chairman of the council usually changes every year; membership of the committees is regarded as a reward for being a good boy or girl rather than as a tribute to knowledge and ability; and continuity of policy is obtained only by the permanence of the officers, whose driving force and ability is a matter of luck rather than of the judgment of the councillors. A board of a company, when once properly constituted (I admit this does not always happen), has security of tenure and special knowledge of the job in hand and in practice fills its own vacancies. Nepotism and guinea-piggery are not unknown, but a board rarely carries these vices so far as to imperil business efficiency or security. The directors' responsibility both supplements and checks the responsibility of the full-time officers, who can moreover be changed if they are or become unsuitable or incompetent. A board of directors has more freedom of initiative, more elasticity in the adaptation of means to ends, a more urgent interest in economic efficiency, than an elected council. For these reasons, a board of directors, at its best, more commonly develops originality and driving force than a council, though there are of course notable exceptions in both types.

On the other hand, the ownership of a whole town site is a powerful economic monopoly. So long as land in a town is owned by a lot of different owners, a private individual wanting land for any purpose can to some extent choose among them, and has therefore some bargaining power. When it is in single ownership, he must accept the terms of the owner or he cannot do business in the town at all. I think that is far too strong a power to place in the hands of unrestricted private ownership, though there are large privately owned estates where the monopoly is administered with imagination and restraint and the fullest sense of public responsibility.

Public planning control and legislation to deal with compensation and betterment may well remove any serious danger of anti-social exploitation; and for this reason I do not rule out the possibility that some new towns may be built by otherwise unrestricted private enterprise. Conversely, in the case of public enterprise, it should not be impossible for local authorities to set up really capable committees, with some co-opted members having knowledge of estate development, and to give them reasonable permanence of status and freedom from political interference, and power to appoint estate managements selected specially for the job. But I think it would be better still if when a site has been selected, the Ministry or local authority concerned should entrust the development of the site to a specially created body with a board chosen for expert knowledge, business ability and wise social outlook, and able to exercise operative freedom equivalent to that of a private enterprise company. Such a body might be entirely financed by public funds, in which case the benefit of enhanced land value would be available for public purposes either in the new town itself or at the discretion of the Ministry or other promoting authority.

Or the developing body might be constituted as an authorized association employing subscribed share capital entitled to a limited dividend when earned, any surplus being available for public purposes in the new town; the larger part of the finance of development being advanced by the Ministry or local authority on mortgage. This system is of course already familiar in the case of public utility housing societies, which obtain loans either from the Public Works Loan Board or from local authorities. A good deal of housing has been done in both garden cities, and in other places, by such societies. Under section 35 of the Town and Country Planning Act 1932, the Public Works Loan Board may make advances to an 'authorized association'—that is a company or society observing an agreed limit of dividend on subscribed capital. If the proportion of finance that could be advanced under this section were raised to 90 per cent of the valuation, and the Treasury Regulations, which are now needlessly hampering, were revised, this machinery might be usable. There are also powers in the Town and Country Planning Act 1944 (section 20) under which local authorities can make advances to authorized associations for town development.

The question naturally arises: in the light of the financial experience of Letchworth and Welwyn, is it to be expected that private capital will be invested in the building of further new towns? And what are the prospects of the charges on public loans for the purpose being duly met? In considering these questions it must be remembered that the capital required for the purchase of the town site and basic estate development is only a small part of the total expenditure on a town. Much larger sums are invested in the building and equipment of houses, factories and commercial premises, and on the local site work and extensions of public utility services associated therewith; and as such developments occur only as and when there is a demand for them, they produce, in a garden city as elsewhere, a normal return on their cost. The special commercial risk in town building falls on the relatively small amount of capital that has to be spent in advance on buying the site, preparing the town plan, and providing the first units of essential services. The critical factor is the period of time during which the town grows to the point which will cover financial charges on this initial expenditure plus the cost of estate management.

Now the experience of Letchworth and Welwyn shows at least this: that with inadequate capital, and with no canalization of urban development by national and regional planning, new towns could be established at a less cost in private loss and public subsidy (taken together), than that of an equivalent amount of central rebuilding or suburban building for a similar mixture of population. We are now entering upon a period when the course of urban development is likely to be canalized by public planning. National policy is to encourage dispersal of population and industry from congested centres. When this policy is effectively applied, wide stretches of agricultural land will be fenced against suburban sprawl and suburban building. The location of new factories will be guided both by restriction in certain areas and encouragement in others. It is obvious that any such policy must favour and speed up development in the areas where development is permitted.

Let us suppose, for example, that a plan of the type of Sir Patrick Abercrombie's Greater London Plan of 1944 had been prepared and adopted by the authorities concerned early in this century. The spreading of Greater London over the nearer parts of Middlesex, Surrey, Kent and Essex would have been checked; the factories barred from the suburban areas of Greater London would have found other sites, usually within the nearest range of London permitted to them. Letchworth and Welwyn would have grown far more rapidly and would have reached financial equilibrium much earlier. If in the near future the Abercrombie Plan of 1944 is, with necessary modifications, adopted, the greater part of the rural land surrounding London will be reserved permanently for agriculture, and a limited number of locations within the area will be specified for new towns and country town extensions. Any such designated situation has at once far more promising prospects of development. The foundation of new towns becomes a sound business proposition, for public enterprise, for private enterprise, and for combinations of both.

The growth of new towns (and of existing country towns) will be even more rapid when they receive fair play in the allocation of housing subsidies. In the past, as I have shown, the subsidies have been heavily loaded in favour of big cities and congested areas. The theory behind this was that rehousing was not only more costly than new housing, but distinguishable in principle from new housing. The distinction has become more and more shadowy. To-day any housing anywhere is really re-housing. To relate housing subsidies to specific slum-clearance or 'decrowding' schemes, and to grant them only to authorities engaged in re-housing directly connected with such schemes, promotes the siting of housing schemes in uneconomic places. It is the worst of governmental sins in a mixed economy—financial discrimination on the basis of varying costs without any plan or policy to replace the economic checks thereby destroyed. The grading of subsidies according to cost of land encourages excessive exploitation of sites and sends up values just where it is socially desirable that they should fall.

The state housing subsidy should be dissociated from compensation for reduced land values under planning. Its purpose should be to cover the gap between the rent-paying capacity of tenants and the current cost of building in normal areas. New houses, complying with the required conditions as to size, quality and equipment, should receive the same subsidy wherever they may be built and (subject to proper safeguards) whoever builds them. If there is to be any discrimination between areas, then the full consequences of the discrimination should be studied and brought into policy; the loading should be not against, but in favour of new towns and country towns where homes can be provided in the best surroundings within easy distance of work. That leaves the problem of compensation for reduction of density in congested areas as a separate problem; it can only be dealt with, under planning, by grants from a National Compensation Fund as proposed in the Government White Paper on *Control of Land Use* (1944), offset by a system of betterment collection. I cannot discuss here the respective merits of the schemes of the Uthwatt Report and this White Paper. But both are in agreement that without a solution of the problem of compensation and betterment, adequate public control of land use is impossible.[1]

Getting the New Communities Going

As in the future, after a relatively small shortage of buildings is overtaken, nearly all building will be replacement building, it is evident that the creation of new towns and the extension of small country towns must be co-ordinated with the more open redevelopment of congested central districts. This is true whether the new developments are promoted and their sites owned by the Government or great city authorities, or whether they are promoted by private enterprise or authorized associations. In all replanning schemes for built-up areas there will be 'non-conforming' business establishments which must be provided for elsewhere. Needs of extensions of premises, impossible on the spot, will also continue to prompt outward business movements. There are also businesses willing to move out voluntarily if good alternative accommodation for themselves and their workers is offered to them in new towns.

The keys to a dispersal policy are, alongside the positive promotion of new dispersal centres: (a) firmness of the planning administration in restricting as far as possible the settlement or exten-

[1] *Expert Committee on Compensation and Betterment: Final Report* (H.M.S.O., 1942). See also my booklet, *The Land and Planning* (Faber, 1941) for a simplified exposition of the problem.

sion of businesses in congested areas or in areas designated as country belts; and (b) making it as easy as possible for new businesses to start in, and for existing businesses to transfer to, the new reception centres. It follows that in the new towns great attention must be paid to the provision of first class facilities for progressive· industries and other businesses. Not only sites with modern services must be provided, but also, for many businesses, buildings on rental at reasonable rents. Public loans should be available for the provision of such buildings by an appropriate state agency, by local authorities or by authorized associations. Subsidies for factory building are not necessary, nor are rebates of rates. Such methods will very rightly be objected to by other firms in the same industries as inducing unfair competition. But there can be no such objection to compensating a business for its actual cost of removal, nor .to paying the removal costs of transferred workers—which can be done under the Town and Country Planning Act, 1944. Temporary transport might also be provided for workers between their old homes and their new workplaces during the transition period if the building of houses does not exactly synchronize with the building of workplaces.

Oversimplification of the process of dispersal can make it seem easier or more difficult than it really is. The easiest case is that of a firm willing and able to move with the whole of its executive and working staff. In that ideal instance there is no problem; the building of the factory or office premises could proceed simultaneously with the building of the houses for the workers; and on a given D-day the move would take place. Such cases do occur, but they may be rare. More often, a firm will take only a section of its existing labour force with it, and recruit its balance of personnel in the new area. It follows therefore that in addition to the workers actually moving with their employment, there must either be a pool of workers in the new locality, or there must be a parallel movement of workers to the new locality and available for employment there. This is what actually happened at the two garden cities. Many new businesses also were started in the two towns, recruiting their key personnel from any part of the country and requiring houses to be available for them, and taking on the less skilled workers already in or flowing to the locality as and when they wanted them. They had no great difficulty in establishing themselves in this way and I see no reason why there should be any greater difficulty in future new towns—indeed, the difficulty would be less, as under the prospective conditions there would be more assured prospects of future growth, on which both employers and workers could count.

So long as you conceive the process as one of exact synchronization of the movement of individual businesses with their whole personnel, it seems dictatorial and unpractical. But if you see it as it really is—a process of guided but essentially willing movement of firms wanting workers and good working conditions, and of workers wanting employment and pleasant living conditions, with care for an overall balancing of the numbers moving, and for proper anticipation of the requirements in the way of housing, business buildings, and other services—it is an entirely practicable process. If you add to this the provision for temporary travelling facilities for workers when for the time being the movement of firms outpaces the building of houses, or alternatively some advance provision of housing in anticipation of the movement of firms and workers—expedients that were rarely possible for the garden cities—the establishment of new towns becomes that much easier.

The difficulties are perhaps greatest at the very beginning. But they should not be exaggerated. Before any factories or houses are completed there is a phase when the only people on the spot are the original rural inhabitants and the workers of all grades engaged in construction. These together are not a negligible number. The first houses could be let to the workers engaged, and certain to be engaged for some years, in the construction of the town. There is no reason why houses should not also be built for sale or letting to workers in the nearest big centre who are prepared to travel to work; indeed a section of a new satellite town could well act, for a time, as a dormitory suburb or housing estate for the neighbouring centre. It will be found that when in due course local employment becomes available in the new town, some of the dormitory workers will be glad to transfer to such local employment; their families also form a small pool of workers and get jobs in new industries as they come along. Workers in surrounding towns and villages also form part of the pool.

It is to be remembered, also, that in addition to the development personnel, and the people employed in manufacturing industry, there are at least an equal number of persons employed in purely local service businesses. People on the lookout for openings will come to the town and start or go into such service businesses as soon as they can get houses. Just after a war, particularly, there are many people seeking such opportunities. Some will come from congested areas whose population is falling. Some will use their war-damage compensation in new areas instead of going back to the places from which they were bombed out.

The sooner the essential services can be provided in the new town the better. A good deal of development work, covering the first section of the town, with roads, clean paths, electricity, water and drainage, ought to be provided before any population, other than the builders, are invited to the town at all. For the original building force temporary camp accommodation will be necessary; but this should be very temporary, until the first permanent houses are ready for the constructional personnel. There must also be a temporary retail store and canteen, and some sort of social meeting-room or clubroom which can be used in the daytime as a school. Very early, and in advance of full demand, a permanent school should be built; and either a first group of shops or a good general store, prepared to carry stocks which in quantity and variety are somewhat beyond what the immediate turnover justifies. At Welwyn the retail stores was built on a larger scale than was really at first required, and part of the building was used for meetings, plays, dances, cinema performances and other community purposes.

As I have said in describing the experiences of Letchworth and Welwyn, there are inevitable cultural and service shortages during the first phases. But if there are good houses and reasonable roads and paths for getting about, the new residents will find the pioneering life not only tolerable but uniquely enjoyable. All the same I would urge the desirability of providing as many amenities as possible in advance of true economic demand. Many of these will be provided by private enterprise and voluntary effort the moment suitable premises are available. Private traders and professional men are alert to any really promising prospect, even if there is a waiting period before the reward comes. And in a new community voluntary association is almost startlingly in evidence. In almost no time the garden cities had their branch banks, laundries, doctors, dentists, printers and local papers, traders, and service and repair businesses. Most of these were prepared to finance or rent premises just as soon as they could get them.

So it will be in the next new towns. If a little money is allocated for non-remunerative community buildings and sports facilities, at once a lively social life will grow up naturally. The notion, at the moment fashionable, of appointing paid social organizers or cultural leaders, seems to me a bit patronizing. Possibly—though I doubt it—social ambulance workers of that type may be needed in big cities where what Howard called the 'isolation of crowds' has lamed people's associational faculties. In a new community, given the meeting places and playing fields, no artificial stimulus is wanted; societies and clubs of all kinds will spring out of the ground. The one thing the estate might usefully organize is some regular means for introducing to the older residents the new ones as they come in; and even this is best left in the main to voluntary effort. Once people have made effective contact with others of like interests, social life takes care of itself if there are places in which to meet and to do things together.*

Expansion of Existing Country Towns*

It is common sense that a dispersal policy which is to include creating new towns of 30,000 to 50,000, should also include expanding up to a like size existing country towns which have been static or on the downward grade. Here some of the experience of Letchworth and Welwyn is of value, though the conditions will be in many respects different. The problem of making a start seems simpler. We are not faced with the question as to which comes first—the population chicken or the industrial egg. There is already a population, and therefore some pool of workers; and any established town, however small, has shops, churches, schools, cinema, public services. On the other hand, the body undertaking the enlargement of an existing town would not have anything like as clear a field for planning; nor could it prevent much of the increase of land value resulting from its expenditure leaking away to owners and interests already established in the town. The fact that the sitting interests—especially the retail traders—will gain by the expansion of the town ought to make them co-operate with enthusiasm. But a lot of conflicting ideas as to the manner and direction of growth will be held by people of local influence; and the business of expansion will, on the political as well as on the planning side, be more complicated than that of creating an entirely new town. This is not to say it will be less interesting.

A country town which is at present rather too small to provide all the amenities urban people desire, or is declining or in danger of decline, should jump at the opportunity presented by the dispersal policy. Many are well alive to the situation already. But few have the resources or the administrative personnel to handle a big industrial expansion.

The Ministry of Town and Country Planning, along with the Board of Trade as the department concerned with the location of industry, should lose no time in designating the towns suited to be reception areas for dispersal. City corporations faced with the need of decongestion might well enter into arrangements with country town authorities for joint conduct of the developmental operations. A city corporation might itself become the landowner of the site of a new neighbourhood unit designed as an integral part of the country town, and undertake the main development, the provision of a factory estate, and much of the housing.

It seems possible, as an alternative, that the country town authority could become the freeholder of its own extension area, the big city authority undertaking by agreement a housing scheme and perhaps an industrial estate within that area, and contributing to the cost of provision of public services by the smaller authority. Or either authority, or both together, could set up and finance an authorized association to do the whole development. It seems to me likely also that in some cases the initiative might be taken by a local group of business men or a group of building societies willing to provide all or some of the finance for development and for building factories and shops if the authorities concerned will undertake the housing and public services. Where a scheme is needed and no authority or private enterprise body is available, the state should be prepared to set up and finance an appropriate developing body.*

The planned extension, on a comprehensive scale, of an existing small town will require the skilled work of a good team. It should begin with a physical survey of the existing built-up area and any land on which extension might take place. The kind of survey undertaken at Letchworth and Welwyn would be appropriate. In addition it would be necessary to assemble data as to the present economic set-up and social structure of the town. For this I would not rely on the usual house to house questioning, which looks scientific but is really only of value when it deals with the more simple facts. The survey should be under the charge of a skilled person, but his principal method should be to create a brains trust of well-informed local residents and administrators and to pool their knowledge in a systematic report. This and the technical reports should be made available to the planning team under the leadership of the planning officer or consultant planner for the area, and the projected expansion should fall into place as part of a long-term planning scheme for the town as a whole.

If the extension were undertaken, as part of the dispersal policy, by some joint body or authorized association, it might be convenient, where possible, to treat it as a neighbourhood with a sub-centre of its own. This would enable some part of the new values to be conserved for the scheme. But it is important that the extension should be integrated with the town as a whole, not only technically and architecturally, but socially; and this will require a great deal of skill and judgment.

Local Government and its Boundaries*

There are people who think a programme of urban dispersal nearly impossible in Great Britain unless it is preceded by a radical revision of local government boundaries. I want to contest this view without begging the controversial question whether local government reform is desirable for other reasons. The issue comes up here in this way. A great city corporation, contemplating re-development of its congested areas at lower density, has to provide somewhere for re-locating part of its population and industry. It cannot do so within its existing boundaries, because as a rule they do not extend much beyond the existing built-up area of the city. But by tradition the size of a city's population is one of the chief measures of its importance; a city authority is averse to losing any of its citizens to the area of another authority. Moreover if, as sometimes happens, it builds a housing scheme for some of its own people outside its own area and within the area of another authority, troublesome questions arise as to rate-loss or rate-profit on the local public services, schools, etc., and as to which authority is responsible for non-remunerative amenities.

Again, a city corporation fears that if some of its population and industry move out, the rateable value and the income it can obtain from local rates will fall by a greater amount than it can save in running expenses; and that the reduced population will therefore have to pay higher rates. Strangely enough, the authority of the county area into which the movement would take place has the exactly opposite fear—that it will be put to extra expense for schools and public services for an extra population.

This competition in fears tends to cause the transferred population to be housed by the city corporation in suburban schemes on its own fringe. The corporation has a battle with the adjoining county authorities and usually obtains an extension of its boundaries to take in the new suburbs. But if, under the dispersal policy, the displaced population is to go several miles out to a new town beyond or in a green belt, the extension of the city boundary is not so simple. A detached island administered by a central city some miles off is inconvenient for both parties. On the other hand the county authorities would violently oppose a wholesale extension taking in a big rural area as well as the new town.

Some spokesmen of the great cities argue for a drastic reform which would place wide country belts around the cities under a new type of administration centred in the great cities, the rural and urban districts within these belts remaining as minor authorities. But this would mean the disappearance or drastic truncation of some of the county councils; and the rural and urban district councils also fear that their authority would be less as minor authorities under the city corporations than under the county councils. Feelings are so strong on the subject that I think it may be a long time before any government ventures on a wholesale reform of this kind, particularly as in the complicated urban-rural layout of Great Britain no completely tidy system can be devised. It is probable that changes will occur, but they are likely to be empirical and even inconsistent.

I do not see that this difficulty need obstruct the dispersal policy. No conceivable rearrangement of boundaries would solve the planning problem if authorities continued to think entirely within their boundaries or to take a proprietorial attitude towards their own populations. The conception, for example, that a local council is responsible for housing its own population, which was a great advance when it emerged in 1919, is already out of date. The responsibility is primarily national: and while local autonomy in executive action is vital local authorities should find their pride and satisfaction in the degree of their success as agents of public policy within their areas. Walt Whitman's ambition for a great city, that of being the healthiest and happiest, is not only loftier but more sensible than that of being the nth city of the Empire. There are many signs that city authorities are rapidly changing their outlook on this matter. Conversely, if city authorities are expected to take a less parochial view of their functions, it is a national obligation to see that they are not saddled with crushing burdens as a result. If a city, for the sake of imaginative and humane planning, faces the displacement of some of its own population and industry, it must not be allowed to suffer heavy financial loss thereby.

It should not be assumed, however, that a city would always lose financially by a dispersal policy. City reconstruction in any form, whether at high or low density, will be an expensive process. If high density is adopted, more costly extensions of certain services —particularly of water supply and sewage disposal—will be required, and in most cases rate-expenditure will increase faster than rate-revenue. A low density policy may not produce so high a rateable value, but public service extensions will cost less. Further, the improved working efficiency of the city, due to lower sickness rates, less traffic delays, and other savings only partially reflected in public accounts, will make it worth while for traders and citizens to pay somewhat more in rates. Better workplaces, better housing, better surroundings, are bound up with a rising standard of living, and must be paid for. In business and private life none of us expects to get something for nothing; why should it be otherwise in municipal affairs?

I see no warrant for fear that a city which, over say twenty years, reconstructs at a reasonably low density will in the end find itself with higher rates than if it does so at high density—though in either case its rates may well be higher than if it had not reconstructed at all. But I do see a danger, as I have already said, that if a city tries to rebuild at a greater density than the citizens of to-morrow will accept, an uncontrollable exodus will produce derelict areas, and the city's last state will be worse than its first. The safest policy financially is so to reconstruct the city that a smaller population of all levels of income will be permanently satisfied to live in it.

Again, what is the ground for assuming that a city can expect a surplus of rate revenue on outlying development by extending its boundaries? It might have a small surplus on a middle class suburb, but that would not be so in the case of a predominantly low-rented housing scheme. A city corporation would have a much better chance of getting some contribution towards its reconstruction costs as freeholder of a new daughter town than as the rating authority for the area. And if prestige and concern for the welfare of the dispersing citizens are at issue, the parent corporation, as the landowner of the whole town site, would have the major say in the development and governance of the daughter town, while it could share the statutory planning powers with the authority for the area by means of an *ad hoc* joint planning committee under section 40 of the Act of 1944. If the new town were developed by an authorized association or public corporation financed by the parent city, the administrative ability and energy of members of the municipality would find ample scope on the directorate.

Whether the freehold is owned and managed directly by the municipality, or through an authorized association, the financial prospects would be greatly enhanced if the developing body were allowed by the Ministries to build factories, shops and the larger types of houses for letting. Consent could be given for this, either under the Housing Act of 1936, or under the Town and Country Planning Act of 1944 if the municipality could show that such building is necessary to make ends meet on its central reconstruction and its overspill development taken together. This seems to me the line to pursue. Assuming a guidance of development towards the new towns by judicious planning restrictions elsewhere, those towns would be remunerative long-term investments. In time there should be a surplus revenue on them, not from rates but from the freehold estate and properties therein, which could fairly be applied to the expenses of central redevelopment.

A new town should be constituted a separate civil parish at the outset, and as soon as there is a local population capable of self-government it should be raised to the status of an urban district and elect its own urban district council. In the case of an existing country town which is to be extended, the area of the authority, whether it is an ancient borough, an urban district, or a rural district, should be enlarged to include the intended extension. The town or district council will be responsible for a number of important services, and its enthusiastic co-operation with the developing body, whether that is a local authority, an authorized association, or a private enterprise company, is most important. It was found both at Letchworth and Welwyn that the elected councillors, who were of all parties, were throughout progressive (though of greatly varying ability) and never held back from any contribution within their powers. The interest of residents in the good development of their town is so great that I think this co-operation could be counted on in future schemes.*

Active help from the county council is also indispensable, and assurances that it would be forthcoming might reasonably be sought when a scheme is initiated. Something more than the provision of services when there is sufficient population to justify them is necessary. There should be some anticipation; otherwise there will be difficulty in getting a new town started. In the long run a prosperous new town in a county area is an asset to the county, but for some years the cost of the services provided—as for example schools, police and main roads—may not be fully covered by the county rates received from the new development. A canny or hard-up county might for these reasons be inclined to go slow on the provision of indispensable services. This difficulty should be overcome if the county council can be convinced that the successful establishment of the new community is assured by planning policy or the energy and resources of the promoting body. In many rural areas, the alternative to new towns and country town extensions is an overall population decline. A county council which realizes this will wish to assist such developments provided the risk of doing so is not excessive.

The Technique of Town Development

My final point is a most important one. I have suggested that new towns, and country town extensions, may be undertaken by a variety of bodies: private enterprise, the state, local authorities, and intermediate and combined agencies. I may seem to have assumed that any of these possesses the necessary knowledge and ability. But this is far from being the case. It cannot be said that local authorities have in general handled even housing schemes in a first-class manner. Many fall short of what we should desire in one or more respects: their layout, their architecture, their planting, their social amenities—even their standard of construction. The record of the private estate developer is certainly no better on average: some extremely good estates are offset by a vast mass of mediocre ones and some execrable ones. The creation of entire communities is a far bigger and more complex task than the building of housing schemes or suburban estates. We are entering upon an era of large-scale development and redevelopment under unified ownerships. That gives us a real chance of producing far better towns than could possibly be produced by unco-ordinated small-scale builders—far better towns even than can be produced by individual enterprise regulated by statutory planning. But the chance cannot be seized unless the work is placed in the hands of skilled estate developers and estate managers, operating plans prepared by adequate technical teams.

This is one of my main reasons for writing this book. Reading my recital of the experience of Letchworth and Welwyn will not turn a chairman of a housing or planning committee, nor even a builder or a council surveyor or an architect, into an expert on town development and management. But I hope it may show the importance, the depth and the complexity of the subject, as well as its fascinating interest. I shall be glad if it leads people who are going to take responsibility for initiating schemes on a large scale, in new towns or old, to see that the enterprise is not one for the amateur, or for the narrowly specialized technician without social interests or experience; and also if it leads technicians to realize that in a job of this magnitude they need the close co-operation of other technicians, of business men, and of men versed in public affairs. It is also most necessary that some of the people who are going to be responsible for town development and redevelopment shall absorb the experience gained at Letchworth and Welwyn and other good large-scale estates, and that men who have taken part in the development and management of such estates should hand on their experience to others. Technical knowledge of the highest order will go astray unless it is associated with the practical 'know-how' which can only be transmitted personally from man to man.

We have in this country excellent schools of architecture and university courses in statutory town planning and estate management. We need in addition schools or university courses in Town Development—a different subject, requiring its own aptitudes and training. The study of the subject would be greatly facilitated, and given reality, if such a school were located in a town where the land is in single ownership, where the best kind of development has already taken place and is still in progress, and where unified administration is in being. Welwyn Garden City (the later of England's two demonstration towns) is the obvious place for it. It is mid-way between the universities of London and Cambridge. Letchworth, the first completely planned modern town, and a number of typical old country towns, are within easy reach, and so is London, full of good examples and awful warnings—from its ducal and crown estates to its crowded slums and sprawling suburbs. Post-graduate courses in such a school, under able direction, using not only the local experience and current practice, but also comparable experience from other estates in Great Britain and abroad, would do much to raise the standard of town development both in the new areas to which industry and population will be dispersed, and in the city centres that have to be rebuilt, and to enable us to make the best use of the great opportunities now opening before us.*

APPENDICES

Appendix I

THE GREEN-BELT PRINCIPLE

A Note on Its Historical Origins

The term *Garden City*, as adopted and defined by Ebenezer Howard, means as much 'a city *in* a garden' as 'a city *of* gardens'. This is clear enough from the nature of his proposals, but he makes it doubly clear in the passage in his book where he says that a garden city which builds over its agricultural belt would thereby forfeit its right to the name. Indeed one of the truly distinctive elements in Howard's scheme is this one—the limitation of the spread of towns, and their permanent separation, by zones of country land generally immune from building.

When describing his scheme as a 'combination' of previous proposals, Howard modestly attributes this country-belt component to James Silk Buckingham, who in 1849 had proposed the building in England of a town of 1,000 acres and 25,000 population, surrounded by an agricultural estate. But this gives too much credit to Buckingham and does not bring out the real advance in thought that Howard made on the great issue of the town and country pattern. Neither Buckingham, nor so far as I can discover any other writer, except Sir Thomas More (who projected an abstract ideal rather than made a practical proposal), clearly anticipated Howard's principle of country belts permanently reserved against the expansion of the towns which they adjoin and surround.

Foreshadowings of the idea, however, are many. Perhaps the oldest is in the layout prescribed for the Levitical Cities of Palestine (*c.* 13th Century B.C.):

'And the Lord spake unto Moses . . . saying, Command the children of Israel, that they shall give unto the Levites . . . cities to dwell in: and pasture lands for the cities round about them. . . . And the cities shall they have to dwell in: and their pasture lands shall be for their cattle, and for their substance, and for all their beasts. And the pasture land of the cities . . . shall be from the

167

wall of the city and outwards a thousand cubits round about.'
(Numbers 35: v. 1–4.)

Later verses give conflicting dimensions, but the pattern is clear:
'the city being in the midst' (v. 5). There are several other refer-
ences in the Old Testament (e.g. 1 Chron. 6 and 13; Joshua 21)
to these Levitical cities. They are described in Numbers as 'forti-
fied and very great'. Greatness is a relative term. Some have been

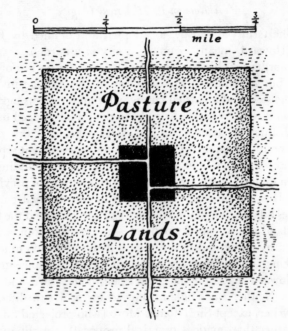

Diagram of a typical Levitical city derived from description in Numbers 35,
and the modern excavation of Gezer. Town area about 22 acres; pasture lands
(permanently reserved) about 300 acres.

identified and excavated; Gezer, one of the largest, had a town
area of 22 acres. Its rural belt, on a reasonable interpretation of
Numbers, was about 15 times the town area. And the belt was
inalienable:

'The field of the suburbs (pasture lands) of their cities may not
be sold: for it is their perpetual possession.' (Leviticus 25: v. 34.)

That this idea of pasture lands around a town was deeply
rooted is evidenced by the proposals of Ezekiel for the layout of

Jerusalem seven centuries later (592–570 B.C.). I confess I would not like the job of planning a city on the specification in Ezekiel 45; the dimensions are so out of scale with the geography of Palestine that I think the translators guessed 'reeds' (which they italicize as uncertain) for 'cubits'. If we substitute cubits, the Holy City works out at the plausible size of just over 1½ miles square, with a perimeter belt (a sort of 'urban fence') 450 feet wide around it, and beyond, on the east and west, 'food lands' extending for another 3½ miles, and on the north vast open areas, nearly 7 miles square, reserved for the Holy Oblation, the Sanctuary, and the farmlands of the Levites.

A century and a half later (c. 444 B.C.), Nehemiah's account of his rebuilding of the walls of the Holy City, on his spell of leave from captivity in Persia, shows that these agricultural reservations were still respected. The intervening dispersal into the surrounding areas was regarded as a fall from grace—except that the 'singers' seem to have been privileged to live in villages outside the city (Nehemiah 12).

Whether Moses, and later Ezekiel, were systematizing an even older tradition, and whether it was held by other races than the Jews, I do not know. But I doubt if anyone in history came closer to practical anticipation of Ebenezer Howard than they did.

The Greeks accepted in theory and practice the limitation of the population-size of a city-state—but that is not the same thing. The idea of a limit of population goes far back; it was held by Lycurgus of Sparta (c. 820 B.C.) and Solon of Athens (640–58 B.C.) Plato (428–347 B.C.) evolved the formula of 5,040 families (not counting retainers and slaves), and was criticized by Aristotle (384–322 B.C.) for putting the figure too high: 'Plato's city would require a territory as large as Babylonia' (Pol. II, 6). Both were thinking of the population of the entire city-state, including the non-urban farmers. Plato, it is true, wanted the city in the centre of the related country; and Aristotle said that it should have open land on one side (the east). Aristotle, moreover, publicized the town-planning theories of the architect Hippodamus (born 480 B.C.) which were not unlike those of the Levites (Pol. II, 8). In view of the population-limit of Greek theory, the mere physical extent of an urban area would not become embarrassing—the impetus to hive off came rather from the limit of the food-raising capacity of the state domain. I see no sign, in the Greek or Graeco-Macedonian town plans, of any reservation of a country belt; though that is only negative evidence that nothing corresponding to the Levitical town pasture lands existed.

The Roman *Pomerium* and *Ager Effatus* imply a tradition that a city should have limits, the extension of which is to be regarded as a rare, grave and deliberate public act, not a casual and private

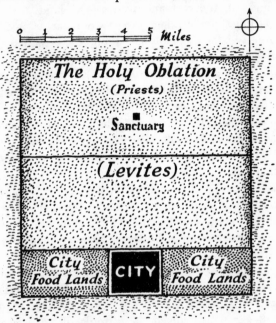

Layout of Jerusalem and its permanent rural reservations as prescribed in Ezekiel 48 but using 'cubits' instead of 'reeds' for all dimensions.

process. The *Pomerium* was a space on both sides of the city walls, kept clear of building and cultivation, and solemnly dedicated so that encroachment should be checked by sentiment as well as law. The military utility of such a space is obvious; but I don't think it is the whole explanation of the tradition, the origin of which is believed to be Etruscan. The *Ager Effatus* (Designated Field) was a belt of open space quite distinct from the *Pomerium*, and extending outside it; and two different sorts of auspices were held in the two zones. If the city were enlarged, a new *Pomerium* line had to be marked out with all solemnity by a plough hauled by a bull and a cow, and the intervening space had to be de-consecrated before it could be built on. On the face of it, this very sensible procedure might seem to provide for the city limitation and urban-rural relationship aimed at by Howard's country belt. But the *Pomerium*, admirable in itself, was only a thin ribbon round the city, and the *Ager Effatus* does not appear to have been reserved against suburban building.

Throughout the records of civilization there is a distinction between 'country' and 'town', and between farming (or 'husbandry', as farming is usually termed in English literature) and the other pursuits of man, most of which implied settlement in closer groups. With few exceptions, until recent times, townsmen retained rural economic interests; a trader or a craftsman usually cultivated land inside the town and just outside it; a 'husbandman' often had a smallholding inside a town and a larger holding or grazing rights outside. The 'cities' of the classical age and of the Bible, the manorial villages of the middle ages, and the walled towns of the Renaissance, do not differ in this respect.

In many cases citizens who engaged (perhaps part time, or part of the family time) in 'husbandry' shared the right of grazing animals on common land adjoining the town. The stormy history of the land laws, among the Hebrews, the Romans, and the people of medieval and modern times, exhibits the same fundamental conflict between the tendency of the rulers or the enterprising wealthy to enclose and increase the productivity of common lands and to dispossess small holders and merge little plots into larger ones, and the reverse tendency of the masses to break up big estates in order to get their 'two jugera' ($1\frac{1}{4}$ acres) or their 'three acres and a cow'. Popular sentiment was always jealous of the encroachment of buildings on open land near towns, or of its appropriation for the suburban estates of the wealthy. But this is only to say that the desire for the urban country-belt is persistent; it is not to say that there was (if we except the Levitical formula) the legal machinery to maintain such a belt in perpetuity.

You see the accepted relationship of country to town, the sentiment that it should be maintained, and the absence of means for its maintenance, in the history of the colonizing movements: in classical times from the Phoenicians to the Romans; in the Middle

Ages from Alfred (A.D. 871–900) to Edward III (A.D. 1327–77), and their Adriatic contemporaries; and in the modern colonial period from the Portuguese settlements, through the great British expansion, down to Balbo's plantations in Cyrenaica. Towns were promoted by the simple expedient of granting smaller sections to colonists in areas designated as urban from those granted in country areas. In Wakefield's famous scheme of 1830, the town section was one acre, and the country section 100 acres; the ratios varied over the twenty-five centuries, but the principle seems to have been general. The Greeks and Romans anticipated the modern practice of granting to the same colonist one town section and one country section as a combined 'lot'—which gave urban folk a certain interest in preserving a balanced relationship of town and country; an interest which, however, always collapsed at the chance of selling out suburban land for building as the new towns grew.

Not all colonial systems deliberately fostered towns. The Dutch colonists in South Africa were granted large rural areas and directed to place their dwellings in the middle of their lots, not in towns or villages; producing the pattern of life described by Olive Schreiner, and perhaps incidentally a conflict of ideologies with later industrial colonists that may have been at the root of the Boer Wars. The different patterns of society produced by the different patterns of urban-rural land-use also underlay the Civil War in the United States.

Another foreshadowing of the idea of the town and its country belt may be traced in the literary Utopias. Plato was the fountain-head of this stream; though he did not specify a country belt, the conception of the limitation of the growth of cities, on its political-economic side, is implicit in his analysis of city structure.

Sir Thomas More's *Utopia* (A.D. 1515–16) closely approaches Howard's garden city pattern. The fifty-four cities of Utopia were twenty miles or more apart, and there is both a distinction and a relationship between town and country, the townsmen being skilled in 'husbandry' and joining in harvesting, and the farmers coming into the city at monthly intervals. The chief city is two miles square, walled, and with a sort of *Pomerium* around the walls —not for military purposes, since it is overgrown with briars, etc., but as an intermediate zone between town and country.

More makes a great point of city children having access to the country and understanding farming from youth: 'partly in the country nigh the city, brought up as it were in playing, not only beholding the use of it, but by occasion of exercising their bodies practising it also'. He is against suburban sprawl. If the population

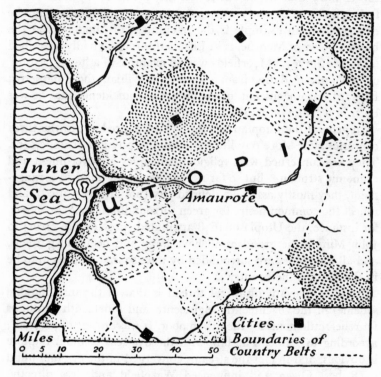

Diagram of an area of Sir Thomas More's Utopia.

of a city grows beyond its capacity, the Utopians do not increase density or build over the large back gardens that More gives to all the houses; they 'fill up the lack in other cities'. If all the towns are full, they 'build up a town . . . in the next land where the inhabitants have much waste and unoccupied ground'.[1]

---

[1] It is chastening to note that More, writing when England was actively settling overseas colonies, supports the *Lebensraum* theory. His Utopians 'detest and abhor' war as 'a thing very beastly'. 'But they count this the most

Incidentally, More also anticipated Howard by dividing his cities into neighbourhoods, each with its minor centre, and by his advocacy of communal feeding.

The value of the country belt to the Utopians is not only economic; More tells us that they 'walk abroad in the fields, or into the country that belongeth to the city'. The strength of urban feeling on the subject of access to the country in all times cannot be exaggerated; an example is the resentment of Londoners at the building-over of Moorfields in Elizabeth's reign, vividly described in Stow's Survey. (Moorfields was an example of a 'town pasture' or 'town moor', dating from a Charter of William the Conqueror; Howard was unconscious of the historical coincidence that he was born in a house on its site.)

In general the Utopian schemes which poured out in the three centuries after More pay little attention to physical arrangement. They are concerned with religion, principles of government and economic structure. But so far as they deal with physical arrangement, they mostly assume a defined city (not always walled), and reflect the common desire for green surroundings. In *Nova Solyma*, for instance, the Utopia of 1648 attributed (probably in error) to John Milton, the grandees all have large and beautiful gardens, and all the houses are surrounded by trees so that 'you seem to be in the heart of the country'.*

Another relevant historical thread is that of the innumerable schemes of the seventeenth, eighteenth and nineteenth centuries for relief settlements for the urban poor. It was an 'age of projects', according to Defoe. The link with the overseas colonial impulse is obvious, and in fact the streams converged in the original mind of Robert Owen and influenced Wakefield and, less directly, Howard. The classic 'project' in this class is John Bellers' *Colledge of Industry* (1696); a scheme for settling 300 to 3,000 people in an industrial community in the English countryside. Here the country-belt idea is implied but not specified.

Among the many others there was the *Proposal for a considerable Number of People to joyn in the Purchas of several thousand Acres of*

just cause of war, when any people holdeth a piece of ground void and vacant to no good nor profitable use, keeping others from the use and possession of it, which notwithstanding by the law of nature ought thereof to be nourished and relieved.'

Drein'd and Derelict Lands, by 'R.S.' (1726), which after quoting Virgil goes on:

'Our first Parent was created in a Garden, and we his Descendants have a natural Bent that way, all Mankind shew by their Actions, that Gardening and a Country Life, are the Objects of their Love and Esteem; Vast Sums by Kings, Princes and Noblemen are laid in Gardening, and when they are glutted with the fulsome cloging Pleasures of Populous Cities, and seriously think of what they had been doing (at least those who ever think to serious purpose at all) retire to their Rural Seats, to meet there, what Crowds of Men in Courts and Cities could never afford them. And nothing but fatal Necessity, depraved Appetite or corrupt Nature, can give us a distaste of innocent Rusticity.'

The author makes the point (of interest to-day) that the settlement of a large number of people on reclaimed land would bring prosperity to 'Neighbouring Towns, a greater Consumption for their Products, and more Imployment for their Poor'. This consciousness of the economics of the urban-rural relationship runs through most of the 'projects' of that time.

My reference to the agitation about Moorfields recalls the successive proclamations and Acts, from Elizabeth to the Commonwealth, prohibiting the suburban expansion of London. These were partly intended to protect the City against the competition of suburban business centres—a battle which the City lost to Westminster and Holborn by the calamity of the Fire of 1666. But another stimulus was the citizens' resentment at the loss of their access to the countryside, of which there is literary evidence extending over centuries. The sentiment in favour of a country belt is always there, though the means of satisfying it is always absent.

We come to Robert Owen, that singular personality, propagandist of so many unrealizable schemes that he may almost be described as Britain's arch-crank, and yet a man who lodged such great ideas in the mind of the world that he is himself almost a turning-point in history. His importance to planning is that he was the first manufacturer to detect that modern industrial technology does not necessitate the aggregation of people in large towns. His mistake was that he did not distinguish physical grouping from economic integration; and this was the point on which Howard made a decisive advance on him.

Owen's proposal of 1817 for small industrial towns in permanent contact with the countryside was not very different from that of Bellers (whom he quotes); but it came at a more appropriate moment. Steam engines had been widely applied to factories from 1785; the Napoleonic Wars ended in 1815; a vast growth and reshuffling of population and industry were in progress. What would have happened if Owen, the successful manufacturer and factory reformer, had not been bitten with separatist communism by contact in America with the Rappites and other religious communities? His gift of getting things done was such that he could achieve anything but the impossible. His economically self-sufficient community failed because it was contrary to immensely powerful economic trends.

Yet both the economic and the physical pattern had an enormous popular appeal. Marx and Engels, men very much alive to working-class opinion, always assumed that large towns were an evil—one of the inhuman corollaries of capitalism—and that after the Social Revolution industry would be diffused through the countryside. They had little sense of town-structure. (See the *Communist Manifesto* of 1848, and Engels' *Condition of the Working Classes in England*, 1844, and *The Housing Question*, 1872.) Owen had a clearer structural idea. If he had concentrated on the physical pattern, and developed his anticipation of Howard's 'town-country magnet', the whole history of urban development in the nineteenth century might have been different. As it turned out, the failure of his self-contained communities discredited his conception of the small industrial town organically related with agriculture, which was inherently sound and practicable

The fact that Owen's ideas were copied by the brilliant madman Fourier, who coupled the continental habit of philosophical systematization with popular journalistic gifts, further confused the issue of the town and country pattern. Buckingham (1849) seems to me to fall into place as a rather more respectable follower of Owen. It was left to Howard in 1898 to disentangle the physical and institutional from the economic factors in the urban problem.

Edward Gibbon Wakefield, in his *Colonization Plan* of 1830, combined some of the theories of Owen and his predecessors with the practice of colonial settlement. He much influenced the new towns of South Australia and New Zealand. This affiliation, in one way or another, probably accounts for the deliberate planning of Park Belts for Adelaide (founded 1837), Wellington (1840), Dunedin (1844), and Christchurch (1847).[1] But the direct inspiration for these Park Belts has, so far as I know, never been traced. Wakefield developed the idea of controlled town-organization; he struggled (successfully) against the diffusion of colonists over larg' areas, which had produced a necessity for indentured labour or slavery. The need of deliberate grouping led to his proposal for colonial companies to dispose of lands, and the coming into being of these land companies produced the administrative powers which made initial town-planning possible—though it did not preclude the subsequent perversion of the plans, as Howard's leasehold system did.

Col. William Light went out to place and plan the capital city of South Australia (1837). He was a man of culture, an artist of distinction, and 'the best gardener in Australia'. He it was who gave Adelaide the famous park belt. Was he told by his Company to do so? I can find no proof of this, though he was asked to reserve adequate open spaces and strips 100 feet wide along the coast and 66 feet wide along rivers and lakes. Was the park belt an inspiration of his own? And was it just a following of his precedent that prompted the New Zealand Company in July 1839, to give these instructions to Capt. Smith, R.A., when he left London to found Wellington?——

'In forming the plan of the town, you should make ample reserves for all public purposes, such as a cemetery, a market place, wharfage, and probable public buildings, a botanical garden, a park, and extensive boulevards. It is, indeed, desirable that the whole outside of the town, inland, should be separated from the county sections by a broad belt of land, which you will declare that the Company intends to be public property, on condition that no buildings be ever erected upon it.

'The form of the town must necessarily be left to your own judgment and taste. Upon this subject the Directors will only

---

[1] Even in New Zealand, in those days, planning was not a highly cultivated art. The surveyor who laid out Christchurch sketched his town plan with his pipe dipped in a mug of beer, which when dry was considered a good working drawing. If this was statutory plan No. 1 for Christchurch, maybe the subsequent evaporation of the park belt can be blamed on the high flashpoint of 1847 ale.*

remark, that you have to provide for the future rather than the present, and that they wish the public convenience to be consulted, and the beautiful appearance of the future city to be secured, so far as these objects can be accomplished by the original plan— rather than the immediate profit of the Company.'[1]

Possibly the idea of the park belt had developed over a period. In the settlement of New South Wales, the Crown had instructed Governor Macquarie (1809) 'to cause a proper place in the most convenient part of each township to be marked out for the building of a town sufficient to contain such a number of families as you shall judge proper to settle there, with town and pasture lots convenient to each tenement'. Later (1810) Macquarie was told that the plan must conform to the 'model supplied', and that a large common must be reserved, nearby, for grazing. I have not been able to find this 'model plan', which applied to the projected townships of Windsor, Richmond, Pitt Town, Wilberforce, Castlereagh and Liverpool. Earlier even than this (1792) Governor Phillip had reserved from sale or lease all land within a certain distance of Sydney, and in 1811 Macquarie enclosed this land for grazing, at the same time creating a common of 1,000 acres one to two miles from the city, for the benefit of the citizens 'for all time'. (Where is it now?)

The practice of the founders of these towns in Australia and New Zealand seems to show two things: (a) that there was a widespread desire, and indeed a traditional assumption, that a town should have unbuilt-on country land nearby; and (b) that in the first flush of disgust at the squalid urban growths of the Industrial Revolution people were particularly conscious of the amenity value of nearby country. But who crystallized part of this idea in the park belts of Adelaide and the New Zealand cities has I think never been elucidated. It may have been Light, but he does not justify or expatiate on the principle in his *Brief Journal* (1839), which makes me wonder if he took it over *per incuriam* from some enthusiast for the idea in England.*

That the park belts in Australasia were a casual inspiration rather than a settled principle is certainly suggested by subsequent history. In the 41 square miles of the suburbs of Adelaide in 1917, only 200 acres had been reserved for public open space; and

[1] *Information Relative to New Zealand*, John Ward, 1841.

First 28 Under New Towns Acts 1946-1968

Melbourne, which had no less than 21 per cent of open space within a 3-mile radius, had only 1½ per cent in the suburbs outside that radius. Christchurch sold some of its park belt for railway and other purposes. Brisbane disposed of much of its open town-lands in the same way.

Clearly there is scope for a much fuller assembling of the evidence from history than I have been able to undertake. The examples I have produced show that Howard's conception of a designated country belt around a town answers to an almost eternal senti-ment or desire, and has an ancestry of partial formulation. But it does not disclose any complete prototype. Howard, I think, was the first to unite Plato's conception of the population-limit, More's principle of adjusting by short-distance migration the balance of population in urban areas, and the universal sentiment for a country setting for a town, into a clear formula; and certainly he was the first to devise and put into operation a land system that could not only establish it but maintain it. It may be that the development of public land-use planning will supersede his effec-tive technique of planning through quasi-public ownership. But it is far from doing so yet. In any case his contribution, which was not merely theoretical but issued in action, stands as decisive.

Appendix II

A NOTE ON TERMINOLOGY

Garden City. Use of this term as a picturesque *sobriquet* of particular cities goes far back. Chicago (surprising as it seems at a distance) called itself The Garden City, through pride in its magnificent surroundings. Christchurch, founded in 1850, was known as the Garden City of New Zealand. The first place to be given Garden City as its official name appears to have been the New York suburb on Long Island started by Alexander T. Stewart in 1869. By 1900 there were, besides this one, nine villages and a small town in the United States named Garden City; how many there are now I do not know. Howard was unconscious of the Long Island use of the name when he adopted it. Its world-wide currency is due to his book; and the term as descriptive of a type of urban settlement should only be used in the sense which he gave to it. A short definition was adopted, in consultation with him, by the Garden Cities and Town Planning Association in 1919:

'A Garden City is a Town designed for healthy living and industry; of a size that makes possible a full measure of social life, but not larger; surrounded by a rural belt; the whole of the land being in public ownership or held in trust for the community.'

Garden Suburb, Garden Village. In these combinations the word Garden connotes simply a well-planned open layout. It is misleading, though good authorities have been guilty of the practice, to describe a Garden Suburb as a suburb 'laid out on Garden City lines'. The word Suburb is conveniently reserved for an outer part of a continuously built-up city, town, or urban area, implying that it is not separated therefrom by intervening country land. Thus a district so placed, and containing, besides dwellings, businesses serving only the local population, should be termed a Dormitory Suburb, or Residential Suburb; and one so placed having industry as well, an Industrial Suburb. However well planned, such a place is wrongly called a Garden City or Satellite Town. The word village implies small scale, detachment, and (I suggest) a basis which is primarily agricultural. Garden Village has been used as a name for a small settlement containing a fac-

181

tory and an associated openly-planned housing estate; it should not however be used generically for such settlements if in a suburban situation.

Satellite Town. This term was first used in Great Britain in 1919 as an alternative description of Welwyn Garden City—a true Garden City in its scale, detachment, layout, structure, and basis of local employment. The reasons for adopting the new term were: first, the prevalent misuse of Garden City as synonymous with Open Suburb or Garden Suburb; second, recognition of a special economic linkage with Greater London. Some planning writers have thoughtlessly renewed the old confusion by using the term Satellite Town to describe an Industrial Garden Suburb. It is better reserved for a Garden City or country town, at a moderate distance from a large city, but physically separated from that city by a Country Belt.

Country Belt, Agricultural Belt, Rural Belt. These terms are synonymous. They describe a stretch of countryside around and between towns, separating each from the others, and predominantly permanent farmland and parkland, whether or not such land is in the ownership of a town authority.

Green Belt. Originally used by Unwin as a further synonym for Country Belt, this term has also been applied, thus far confusingly, to a narrow strip of parkland more or less encircling part of a built-up metropolitan or large urban area. Park Belt is a better name for such a strip.

Decentralization, Dispersal, Diffusion. Till recently advocates of the Garden City idea have used Decentralization as the keyword for the planned movement of people and workplaces from congested urban areas to detached smaller towns. In America it is often used to mean the spontaneous movement from the centre to the immediate outskirts of an urban area—quite a different thing. Lately the word Dispersal has been adopted for the former process; and this usage is now becoming standardized. As a planning term it definitely does not connote a wide spreading of development over rural areas. For this latter process, if a technical label is needed, it is better to use the term Diffusion. Decentralization remains available as a general term for any outward movement; but for the combined settlement of both industry and residents in suburbs I suggest the word Sub-Centralization.

Appendix III

'The Company has been formed to develop an estate of about 3,800 acres, between Hitchin and Baldock, on the lines suggested by Mr. Ebenezer Howard in his book, *Garden Cities of To-Morrow*, with any necessary modification.

'The root idea of Mr. Howard's book is to deal at once with the two vital questions of overcrowding in our towns and the depopulation of our rural districts, and thereby reduce the congestion of population in our great towns, or at least arrest its progress.

'The advantages anticipated from this new departure in the development of a building estate are: Firstly, the provision of hygienic conditions of life for a considerable working population. Secondly, the stimulation of agriculture by bringing a market to the farmer's door. Thirdly, the relief of the tedium of agricultural life by accessibility to a large town. Fourthly, that the inhabitants will have the satisfaction of knowing that the increment of value of the land created by themselves will be devoted to their own benefit.'

Extracts from Statement of the Provisional Board of Second Garden City, 1919.

'A SATELLITE TOWN FOR LONDON.

'The object of the Company will be to build an entirely new and self-dependent industrial town, on a site twenty-one miles from London, as an illustration of the right way to provide for the expansion of the industries and population of a great city. Though not the first enterprise of the kind (the main idea having already been exemplified at Letchworth), the present project strikes a new note by addressing itself to the problems of a particular city. To this end the site has been carefully chosen so as to minimize the obstacles in the way of giving a new turn to the development of Greater London. . . .

'It is urgently necessary that a convincing demonstration of the garden city principle of town development shall be given in time to influence the national housing programme, which is in danger of settling definitely into the wrong lines. Unless something is done to popularize a more scientific method of handling the question, a very large proportion of the houses to be built under the national scheme will be added to the big towns—whose growth is already acknowledged to be excessive.

'Garden suburbs are no solution. They are better than tenements, but in the case of London they have to be so far from the centre that the daily journeys are a grievous burden on the workers. . . . And this method ignores the needs of industry. Manufactures carried on in makeshift premises in Central London cannot hope to be efficient or to meet either the legitimate demands of labour or the renewal of international competition.

'The Company's scheme, therefore, will pay equal attention to housing and to the provision of manufacturing facilities. Healthy and well-equipped factories will be grouped in scientific relation to transport facilities, and will be equally accessible from the new houses of the workers. . . .

'The town will be laid out on garden city principles, the town area being defined, and the rest of the estate permanently reserved as an agricultural and rural belt. . . . A population of 40,000 to 50,000 will be provided for, efforts being made to anticipate all its social, recreative and civic needs. The aim is to create a self-contained town, with a vigorous life of its own independent of London.

'The freehold of the estate will be retained in the ownership of the Company (except in so far as parts thereof may be required for public purposes) in trust for the future community. The preservation of the beauty of the district, and the securing of architectural harmony in the new buildings, will be among the first considerations of the Company.

'From the national standpoint an important feature of the whole scheme is its influence upon the agricultural community. Not only does it provide openings for many additional workers on the land, but (unlike other methods of rural reform) it brings the advantages of a vigorous urban social life within the reach of the agricultural population.'

NOTES TO NEW EDITION

NOTES TO NEW EDITION

On each page to which the notes refer, the relevant paragraph is identified by an asterisk (*)

Page 13. It is interesting to note in this opening paragraph what I selected in 1945 as the key points in the case against overgrown agglomerations. Though I included the burden of long-distance commuting, I did not mention that of road-traffic congestion. This has now become a far more powerful stimulus to public concern than social compunction ever was. Rather a sad reflection, I think, on our sense of values. And many cities, in their efforts to meet the demands of the car, are actually worsening the human environment.

15 (1). This touching trust extended also to the economists, whose influence increasingly sways all parties. Their occupational tendency is to equate maximum statistical productivity with maximum material welfare. Most even of those who, like J. K. Galbraith, take some account of environmental consequences have failed to appreciate the necessity of planned limits of size as well as density of cities.

15 (2). London has lately resigned from this imbecile competition – the first of the world's great cities to do so (see Note 51,1). It has agreed to the reservation of a green belt to stop the spread of the continuously-built-up area, and to some "export" of its population, though its old slums, when cleared, have in the main been replaced by high flats, and densities have not been reduced anything like enough to permit of the desired proportion of houses with gardens or a reasonable amount of recreation space. The populations of the other major conurbations in Britain are now fairly static, but large increases continue in their surrounding regions.

16. The allegation persists that proponents of new towns think of them as ends in themselves and are indifferent to the task of renewal in existing cities. On the contrary: the latter has always been the primary concern of Howard and his followers.

17. My prediction as to U.S. policy is fulfilled by the New Communities Act of August 1968. The deteriorating state of U.S. cities is complicated by racial segregation and pockets of extreme poverty. Governmental action, when accepted as unavoidable, takes the form of loan guarantees to private enterprise rather than of public promotion and finance. This federal Act of 1968 is a significant move towards an urban dispersal policy. But some leading American advocates doubt if it will work, and are pressing for the setting-up of federal or state corporations with powers to acquire sites in rightly placed locations and to do the groundwork on which industrial, commercial and other buildings can be provided by normal business and housing agencies.

18. I would stress the point in this and ensuing paragraphs. Too many well-disposed supporters of the new towns movement see it merely as a rescue operation for the under-privileged, not for the likes of their cultivated selves. Many of these, not place-bound by their occupations, and many who have retired, are missing the opportunity of a rich personal adventure coupled with a valuable contribution to the social and cultural development of a new community, to the lasting benefit of its character. In time all towns throw up their natural leaders, but it is in the pioneering days that the kind of people I have in mind could be most helpful and find enjoyable interest.

21. Much discussion has recently sprung up on "public participation" in planning. The term could mean the "mobilisation of consent" to what authorities and experts want to do or think best for the dumb masses (see *Essays in Reform,* ed. Bernard Crick, London, 1968). In principle democratic authorities are the servants of the people. In practice urban development is so complex that the servants, while wishing to be loyal to their masters' interests and preferences, have to explain what is practicable and what is not – in which assessment they are themselves conditioned by political circumstances, firmly set but not necessarily unalterable. They can be forgiven for accepting circumstances beyond their influence. But they should watch out that they do not impose their own fads or fashions or theories of a future superior "way of life".

21. The New Towns (Reith) Committee, of which I was a member, reported in 1946 (see my preface, page 2; and for a brief summary of its recommendations, F. J. Osborn and A. Whittick: *The New Towns: The Answer to Megalopolis*, 1963 and 1969).

24. My comment on the planning literature of 1898–1945 remains true of much of the vast output since. Under pressure of economic and electoral pressures of immense strength and limited preoccupations city planners can only assess and forecast (with the aid of computers) and marginally regulate trends. Philosophers of planning have widely differing approaches and subjective valuations. And like economists (Note 15), political theorists of both Right and Left, though in conflict on the issue of free enterprise versus collectivism, are equally disposed to assume that with enough money people can buy what they want, which in the matter of environment is simply not true.

27. Howard has recently been accused in some academic studies of being "anti-urban" – a charge that has been made against nineteenth-century English and American writers in general (see for instance M. and L. White: *The Intellectual Versus the City*, Cambridge, Mass., 1962). The charge is absurd. To be against the evils of great cities is not to be against towns, or against the factory system, or even to be "agrarian" in the Jeffersonian sense. It is particularly absurd to throw it at Howard, who put forward his ideal as "a great and most beautiful city" (see page 49).

29. Though economists and sociologists are not specified by Howard in the planning team, they need not feel cold-shouldered. In the sense that Molière's Monsieur Jourdain was a speaker of prose, Howard was a born sociologist and economist himself.

31. Unified land-ownership and leasehold have since been widely adopted in public and commercial development, notably under the Town and Country Planning Acts of 1944 and 1947, which set a general limit of 99 years on leases by municipalities undertaking redevelopment. Such long leases however do not capture for the public future increases of value. Most of the British new towns have therefore adopted the Welwyn practice (pp. 73, 84–88) of financing commercial buildings and letting them at revisable rack-rents, which has proved of cardinal importance.

32. Top rates of income taxation have since risen to 90% and of death duties to 80%.

NOTES TO NEW EDITION

32 (footnote). The Uthwatt proposals were not adopted. Instead, Silkin's major Planning Act of 1947 provided for compensation for existing building rights or expectations, and the collection of 100% of "development value" if and when building was permitted. Much compensation (a huge sum) was in fact paid, and this has made possible the reservation, without further compensation, of extensive "green belt" areas. But the 100% charge (which discouraged development) was repealed by a succeeding Government, and replaced in 1965 by a charge of 40% (which can be increased to 50%) on increases of value caused by new planning consents for changes of use. I think if Silkin had fixed his charge at 75% or 80% he could have got away with it. But the question remains highly controversial.

33. The subdivision of towns into wards, later ably advocated by Clarence Perry in *The Neighbourhood Unit* (1929), has become a planning orthodoxy, but there are differing opinions as to the appropriate size of these units. In the British new towns they vary in population from about 3,000 to 14,000. For some purposes their practical convenience is obvious, but how far they promote neighbourhood consciousness is debatable. I think that on pages 94–95 I understate their potential value.

34. The economic development of agriculture in organized relationship with a particular town market has not been much pursued, though there was an experiment at Welwyn Garden City (see page 69). I would not now describe the idea as important. Farmers, market-gardeners, distributors and individuals, when near each other, find reciprocal markets spontaneously. A new town livens up its whole surrounding countryside economically and culturally.

36. At the end of 1968 Letchworth had about 28,500 people and Welwyn about 45,000. With their neighbouring towns, at distances of 3 to 7 miles but separated by belts of open country, they had become units in "cluster-cities" of about 150,000 and 100,000 respectively, within which about 90% of the occupied residents had their employment. Many more workers came into Letchworth and Welwyn daily than went out (see *Sample Census, 1966: Workplaces & Transport, Pt. 1, 1968*).

42. The Fog-Blowers and Dust-Throwers have not ceased to perform. Nor have the fantasts. In 1968 the B.B.C. televised a scheme for a complete tower-town of 240,000 two miles high, inspired by the designer's admiration for ant-heaps. This was not meant to be funny. Nor was Frank Lloyd Wright's earlier proposal for a block one mile high, nor Le Corbusier's *Ville Radieuse*, in which human beings were to be housed at 400 to 1,300 an acre in 15–20 storey slabs on stilts, with internal traffic roads and batches of lifts taking 2,400 persons to a single exit door – an incompetently calculated, as well as a heartless plan, even if it were practicable.

45. Satan did not comply. The delusion that new towns would obliterate the countryside persists, despite the demonstrations by Dr. Robin Best (in *Land for New Towns*, London, 1964) and others that at their average density towns for another 10 million people would require not more than 1½% to 2% of Britain's agricultural land. (See Note 146.)

51 (1). This movement led to the Town Development Act of 1952, under which by the end of 1968 over 100 country-town expansions for nearly 500,000 people had been agreed between large and small authorities, and about 200,000 had been housed. Led by London, some large cities are actually contributing financially to the "export" of their excess population, industries and office businesses, with a wise generosity I did not anticipate in 1918 or 1945 (see Note 15, 2).

51 (2). I would now replace "at least fifty" by "very many" (see pages 3–4.)

55. Full histories of Letchworth and Welwyn Garden City have still to be written. My contribution in this book strikes me now as having some value as a source; also as a proto-textbook, because in 1945 I knew by recent experience a lot more about the business of creating new towns than I can remember now.

58. A later change in company law unfortunately made it possible for First Garden City Ltd. to abandon its profit limits without consent of the High Court (see Note 108).

63. Britain's gas and electricity services have since been nationalized, and water supplies transferred to regional statutory companies. In both towns sewers and sewage disposal works have been taken over by the local authorities.

67. Useful data about the choice of trees and their placing and maintenance is to be found in *Landscaping Two Towns*, by M. R.

Sefton, landscape architect of Welwyn Garden City (1962).

69 (1). The Letchworth Garden City Corporation now itself farms 1,000 acres of its agricultural belt.

69 (2). Two alternative sketch plans had in fact been submitted. One of these was by Professor W. R. Lethaby and Halsey Ricardo. They are briefly described by C. B. Purdom in *The Letchworth Achievement* (1963).

71. See my remarks on "know-how" (p. 6).

73. Under the Leasehold Reform Act 1967 owner-occupiers of leasehold houses are now entitled to buy the freehold – a curiously individualistic piece of legislation by a socialist Government. There are, however, provisions for well-maintained estates to establish "schemes of management" to preserve amenities in the public interest.

74. "Local option" in Letchworth has since been abandoned. All the new towns have many licensed public houses.

75. In England unfenced front gardens or forecourts are disliked by the majority of occupiers, but not by all. In this matter consumer demand should obviously be the guide. Very acceptable effects can be obtained by skilful landscaping.

80. Maximum productivity is not the sole criterion of social progress. The effect on the human environment is fundamentally important (see Note 15, 1).

83. The decentralization of office businesses is now officially encouraged. London's Location of Offices Bureau (LOB) urges and helps them to move out, to relieve the central pressure. But the building of lofty towers goes on and new businesses still come in. A more logical and resolute policy is plainly called for. London half-sees a necessity to which most great cities are blind.

87. On the take-over of Welwyn Garden City under the New Towns Act the Welwyn Department Store was sold to a big multiple organization. It has been a factor in making the town a first-class shopping centre – and, incidentally, has magnified its car-parking problem.

88. There were in 1968 six sub-centres, and altogether about 180 shops.

90. For a population of 42,500 (1968) there are about 26 schools with nearly 11,000 places. Some of these are being combined into secondary "comprehensives" as in most English towns.

Other public buildings in W.G.C. include 19 churches, 12 public houses, 8 youth centres, 3 libraries, 7 community halls, a sports stadium (besides many playing fields), an art centre, and a magnificent hospital. A multi-purpose community centre is planned.

92. In the later parts of Welwyn Garden City there has been a tendency to increase housing densities, but not to the extent observable in some other new towns.

93. We made strenuous efforts in Welwyn Garden City to educate the public in architectural appreciation, with some success. For our publicity I invented the slogan "Houses good to look at as well as to live in", with the addendum: "You live in one house, but outside all the others".

95. Neighbourhoods (see Note 33).

102. Front gardens (see Note 75).

103. British Railways, now nationalized, are much more concerned than in those days for the quality and placing of posters.

104. Public services (see Note 63).

106. Under the New Towns Act the W.G.C. Development Corporation exercised the local planning powers. When the estate was taken over by the Commission for the New Towns, the statutory function reverted to the county planning authority. But in both situations there has had to be local consultation and ministerial approval.

108. Garden City finance (see page 106). The two companies did in the end produce substantial surplus profits, though these benefited their shareholders and not, as originally intended, the inhabitants of the towns (see Note 58). When taken over, under different acts, by public corporations, Letchworth yielded its investors a bonus of £2½ million and W.G.C. £1.4 million. But the corporations got good bargains, since revenues and values continue to rise. Whether the national Treasury, which is the legal heir to this fortune, will share it with the inhabitants remains to be seen.

115. The proportion of occupied residents of W.G.C. commuting to London had fallen by 1966 to about 6%½. For Letchworth it was 2½% (Official Census Report, 1968). There is, of course, considerable interchange of workers with neighbouring towns and villages (see Note 36 and page 145).

123. Fewer people in the suburbs of great cities frequent their central cultural facilities than the poster-conscious may suppose. Recent research has revealed that of the residents of the outer suburbs of Paris over 50% never got to a theatre and over 75% never go to an orchestral concert, while another 15% go extremely rarely. Indeed, a third of those questioned had not visited any single one of the leisure facilities of central Paris in a year. There is a sharp fall in such attendances when journey-to-work time exceeds 10 hours a week, as it does for half the suburban commuters.[1]

130. In America the computer has added enormously to the data available to planners. Would they claim that it has much clarified their ideas or enabled them to check inordinate urban growth? They can more precisely predict the trend, but as a leading U.S. planner has written: "Trend is not Destiny".

131. The political evolution of the British dispersal policy, of which by luck I was an inside observer, is dealt with more fully in my chapters of *The New Towns: The Answer to Megalopolis*.

132–133. "Which no planner wants". Perhaps I was too confident here. There are "planners" who, as someone said of the prophet Habbakuk, are capable of anything.

133. The reversal of the population trend modifies much of my argument on pages 133–137 (see page 3).

145 (1). The designations in 1968 for several "New Cities" of 200,000 to 500,000 people are not in principle a breakaway from the garden city concept. But it would be a return to the error of the past if they were planned as solidly built-up aggregations. They should be planned as "cluster cities", interpenetrated by stretches of open land, in the several towns of which most people could live at moderate densities near their work and the countryside. This pattern, as I mention in Note 36, is emerging in the clusters of which the two garden cities are constituents.

145 (2). In general the designated areas of the new towns include very little "green belt" land. British planning powers since 1947 enable the belts to be preserved from development.

146. The number of farm workers in Great Britain has fallen from 887,000 in 1945 to 418,000 in 1968, while tractors in use rose from about 200,000 to 500,000. Farm output in the same

[1] *Espace et Loisir dans la Société Française*. C.R.U., Paris, 1967. (See book list.)

period, in real terms doubled, though the area farmed remained about the same, losses to urban development being offset by the up-grading of rough grazings.

149. Under the New Towns Act full powers of compulsory purchase are given to development corporations, subject to ministerial approval.

149. Agencies for building new towns. The Reith Committee (1945–6) went very thoroughly into the question of possible agencies, and I as chairman of a sub-committee consulted the associations of local government authorities, insurance companies, building societies and builders as to whether any of these would be interested. There was a strong consensus of opinion that it was a task for *ad hoc* development corporations financed by the Government.

159. The planned expansion of country towns has been provided for by the Town Development Act 1952 (see Note 51).

160. The matter of boundaries was referred to a Royal Commission on Local Government in 1967, due to report in 1969. Major issues of regional economic and physical planning and of their co-ordination have arisen, and the new Department of Economic Affairs set up in 1966 economic planning boards and councils for Scotland, Wales and nine regions of England.

164. Friction did inevitably occur between some of the development corporations and local authorities. But on the whole co-operation was effective, since basically they had a common interest in the success of the enterprises.

166. This idea of a School of Town Development was not taken up, and I doubt if there is yet an adequate course on the subject in any university or college. Leadership in the business calls for a liberal education, including a broad acquaintance with economics, social science, law, finance, administration and public relations. Its "technique" is closer to estate management than to statutory planning control, architecture, civil engineering, building construction, or surveying, though all these disciplines are required in the development team.

174. For the history of community projects see W. H. G. Armytage: *Heavens Below* (1961), a fascinating collection, though it does not clearly discriminate between "ideal" conceptions and projects for action. For actual foundations see M. Beresford: *New*

Towns of The Middle Ages; F. Haverfield: *Ancient Town Planning* (1913); Marcel Poëte: *Introduction à l'Urbanisme* (1929); etc.

177. In my joke about the planner of Christchurch, N.Z. I should obviously have blamed the low rather than the high flashpoint of 1847 ale.

178. My study of the Green Belt principle was followed up 15 years later by Professor John Reps ("The Green Belt Concept": *Town and Country Planning*, July, 1960). He traces back the application of it in Australasia to several English writers on colonizing policy, through Granville Sharp (1794) and J. E. Oglethorpe (planner of Savannah, about 1730) to James Mountgomery (1717). I would still like to see the instructions to Colonel Light and the pipe-and-beer planner of Christchurch.

SELECT BIBLIOGRAPHY

SELECT BIBLIOGRAPHY

This selection from the many publications on new towns is intended to be of interest to practical developers of towns, their inhabitants, political decision-makers, and historians of planning, as well as general readers. Some publications which are out of print can be found in public or institutional libraries.

Abercrombie, Patrick: *Greater London Plan 1944*. London, 1945. A masterpiece of historic importance. Later plans, though necessitated by change, are not all advances.

Armytage, W. H. G.: *Heavens Below: Utopian Experiments in Britain 1560–1960*. London, 1961. Rich collection of theoretical ideals and actual experiments.

"Barlow Report": *Royal Commission on Distribution of Industrial Population: Report and minutes of Evidence*. London, 1940. Massive assembly of facts and figures. Proved turning point in planning policy.

Best, Robin H.: *Land for New Towns: a study of land use, densities, and agricultural displacement*. London, 1964. With scientific accuracy, corrects ill-informed alarmism.

Baron, S. (ed.): *Country Towns in the Future England*. London, 1944. Report of T.C.P.A. Conference that opened the campaign for small-town expansion.

Block, G. D. M.: *The Spread of Towns*. London, 1962. A Conservative Party publication supporting dispersal.

Centre de Recherche d'Urbanisme: *Espace et Loisir dans la Société Française*. Paris, 1967. *La Politique Pavillonnaire* (3 vols.) Paris, 1966. Research studies revealing French preferences in housing and environment closely resembling British.

"Chamberlain Report". *Report by Committee on Unhealthy Areas*. London, 1920. First official report to recommend "self-contained garden cities" with industry around London.

Commission for the New Towns: *Annual Reports*. London, 1963 to date. Reports for the towns taken over from development corporations.

SELECT BIBLIOGRAPHY

Conservative Political Centre: *Change and Challenge: Next Steps in Town and Country Planning*. London, 1962.

Garden Cities and Satellite Towns: Report of Departmental Committee (Marley Report). London, 1935.

Creese, W. L.: *The Search for Environment: The Garden City Movement Before and After*. New Haven, 1966. Contains some historical information not elsewhere available.

De Soissons, L., and Kenyon, A. W.: *Site Planning in Practice at Welwyn Garden City*. London, 1927. Good examples of early layout.

Howard, Ebenezer: *Garden Cities of Tomorrow* (1898). Latest edition, ed. F. J. Osborn, with Essay by Lewis Mumford, London, 1965. The book that started the new towns movement. Translations have been published in French, German, Russian, Czech, Italian, Spanish and Japanese.

International Federation for Housing and Planning: *Report of Jubilee Congress, Arnhem, 1963:* on "Bigger Cities or More Cities?" The Hague, 1964.

— *Report of Orebro Congress, 1965*, on "Space Requirements in Planning". The Hague, 1966.

Keable, G.: *Tomorrow Slowly Comes*. London, 1963. A non-academic record containing useful information about history of the T.C.P.A., dates of events, and personalities.

Labour Party: *Towns for our Times*. London, 1961. A booklet endorsing the dispersal policy.

Local Newspapers, etc. All the towns have weekly journals. The Development Corporations issue booklets about their individual towns.

McAllister, G. and E. (ed.): *Homes, Towns and Countryside*. London, 1945. Symposium that had influence in a decisive period.

Mandelker, D. R.: *Green Belts and Urban Growth*. Madison, Wis., 1962. Objective study of British green-belt policy by an American observer.

Mayer, Albert: *The Urgent Future*. New York, 1967. Vigorous argument for drastic urban renewal and regional planning.

Mitchell, Elizabeth: *The Plan that Pleased*. London, 1967. Charming record of new towns movement in Scotland by one of its leaders.

SELECT BIBLIOGRAPHY

Mumford, Lewis: *The Culture of Cities*. New York and London, 1938. Philosophic study, strongly endorsing Howard's garden city concept, as also do the following important books:
—*The City in History*. New York and London, 1961.
—*The Highway and the City*. New York and London, 1963.
—*The Urban Prospect*. New York and London, 1968.
New Towns: *Reports of the Development Corporations* (for England and Wales and for Scotland). London and Edinburgh, 1948 to date. Progress reports and accounts.
Osborn, F. J.: *New Towns After the War*. London, 1918. Revised edition, 1942. Short restatement of Howard's thesis with proposals for national policy.
—*Overture to Planning*. Booklet with introduction by Viscount Samuel. London, 1941.
—*Can Man Plan? and Other Verses*. London, 1959. Humorous and satirical variations on author's more solemn manifestoes.
—"Ebenezer Howard: The Evolution of His Ideas".: article in *Town Planning Review*, October, 1950. Brief character study and assessment of Howard's life and work.
Osborn, F. J., and Whittick, A.: *The New Towns: The Answer To Megalopolis*. London, 1963. Revised edition, 1969. Record of the evolution of British policy and descriptions of first 28 New Towns in progress. Plans, photographs, statistics, and world list of modern planned communities.
Purdom, C. B.: *The Building of Satellite Towns*. London, 1925. Well-documented account of development of Letchworth and Welwyn Garden City.
Riboud, Jacques: *Developpement Urbain: Recherche d'un Principe*. Paris, 1965. Powerful argument for regional groups of new towns in France.
Riley, D. W.: *The Citizen's Guide to Town and Country Planning*. London, 1967. Useful summary for general reader. Revised edition in preparation, 1969.
Rosner, R.: *Neue Städte in England*. Munich, 1962. Favourable study of British new towns and policy.
Self, Peter: *Cities in Flood*. London, 1957, revised 1961. Able advocacy of new towns and regional planning.
Stein, Clarence: *Toward New Towns in America*. Liverpool, 1951, and Cambridge, Mass., 1966. Well illustrated description of

Radburn and Green-Belt Towns in U.S.A., with valuable technical advice.

Stone, P. A.: *Housing, Town Development, Land and Costs*. London, 1963. Expert cost analysis of high-density versus dispersal development.

Town and Country Planning (formerly The Garden City). London, 1907 to date. Now monthly. Running record of movement from start. See especially January (New Towns) issues, 1949 to date.

Town and Country Planning Association (T.C.P.A.). Publications and Statements since foundation in 1899 have been major influence on British policy (See *Town and Country Planning* (journal) and Keable, G.).

United Nations: *Planning of Metropolitan Areas and New Towns*. New York, 1967. Reports of Symposia of Experts, Stockholm 1961 and Moscow 1964.

Unwin, Raymond: *Town Planning in Practice*. London, 1920, reissue 1932. Internationally influential book by this great planner.

Viet, Jean: *New Towns: a selected annotated bibliography* (in French and English). Unesco, N.Y., 1960. List of 790 books and articles in many languages. Useful, but now needs additions. See list of towns in Osborn – Whittick (above).

INDEX

INDEX

Abercrombie, Sir P., 48-50, 63, 143, 146, 152
Adelaide, 177-8
Advertisements, control of, 47, 75, 98, 101, 103, 191
Africa, 51, 172
Ager Effatus, 170
Agriculture, 27, 29, 34, 60, 68-9, 145-8, 192-3; markets for, 33, 34, 175, 183, 184; preservation of land for, 9, 33, 41, 49, 142, 146-8, 171, 189 (See also Green Belts)
Airports, 144
Alberti, 37
Alfred the Great, 172
Allotments and smallholdings, 61, 68, 119, 147-8
Ancient buildings, 30, 41, 50, 138
"Anti-City" attitude, 185, 187
Architecture, 29-30, 37, 48, 51, 64, 69, 88, 103, 165, 184, 191; conflict of styles, 41, 100; fantasies, 9, 43, 47 (See also Design)
Aristotle, 33, 169
Armytage, W.H.G., 193
Asia, cities in, 15, 16, 17, 51
Athens, 37
Australia, cities in, 15, 176-81, 194
Authorized associations, 107, 149, 159, 163

Backward countries, 16, 17, 51
Balzac, H. de, 113, 118n.
Barlow Report, ix, 1, 46, 47, 48, 131
Baron, S., 51n.
"Beiunskis", 43
Bellers, John, 174, 176
Beresford, M., 194
Berlin, 15
Berwick-on-Tweed, 70
Best, Robin H., 189
Bible, cities in, 33, 167-9
Bicycles, parking, 77
Bird sanctuaries, 41, 47
Birmingham, 15, 17, 26, 81, 90
"Bloomsbury" way of life, 19, 20, 125
Bournville, 38, 71

Brussels, 17
Buckingham, J.S., 33, 35, 167, 176
Building, cost of, 109; industry, 29, 93-4, 138, 149; materials, 61, 62; regulations, 61, 74
Building societies, 149

Cadbury, George, 34
Cars and car-parks, 9, 38, 77, 185, 190
Centres, main and minor, 89-90, 94-95, 99, 160
Chamberlain, Neville, 46
Chambers, Sir Theodore, 55
Chesterton, G.K., 19, 20, 68
Chicago, 76, 181
Children, 9, 13-14, 30
Christchurch, N.Z., 177, 181, 194
Churches; buildings, 30, 112, 117, 132, 158; siting, 28, 89, 94, 95; bells, 103; religious life, 120, 123
Cinemas, 89, 123, 127, 157, 158
Cities, see Towns
City renewal, 185
Civic Directors, 58, 105
Class segregation, 42, 91-3, 116
Clubs and societies, 74, 87, 90, 94, 95, 119, 123, 132, 157, 158
Cluster cities, 3, 7, 17, 49-50, 53, 146, 187-8,192
Communist Manifesto, 176
Community life, 7, 48, 80, 94-5, 113-28, 157-8, 160; in small and large towns, 18-20, 26, 49; disintegration of, 13, 42 (See also Class, Cultural)
Commuting, 7, 8, 188
Computers, 187, 192
Compensation and betterment, 32, 48, 151, 153, 188
Conurbations, 15, 185
Co-operative method, 17, 33, 34; movement, 29-30, 85-6, 87, 149
Co-Partnership Tenants Ltd., 39
Country towns, expansion of, 16, 49-51, 81, 131, 133, 137, 153, 158-60, 189, 193

Countryside, access to, 13, 33, 49, 173-5, 183; preservation of, 41, 44, 47, 91 (See also Agriculture)
Crick, Bernard, 186
Cultural life, 7, 19-20, 26, 93, 95, 113-128, 186; facilities for, 28, 157; lack of, 42, 50, 146 (See also Community life)

Dalton, Hugh, 131
Dancing, 119, 157
Democracy and planning, 14, 21, 74, 100, 116, 117, 150, 164
Density, excessive, 13, 25-6, 32, 50; standards, 9, 28-9, 34, 39, 62, 92, 102, 133, 145, 147, 192
Design, control of, 34, 41, 62, 75, 88, 89, 93-4, 98-101, 102, 191 (See also Architecture)
de Soissons, Louis, 71
Development charge, 188
Development corporations, 2, 4, 5-6, 164, 193
Dickens, Charles, 125
Dinocrates, 141
Dispersal; meaning, 131-2, 182; limits, 80-1, 143, 147; methods, 152-60; policy, 32, 48, 111, 112, 131-2; scale, 51, 133-40
Dividend, limitation of, 4, 5, 58, 69, 107, 110, 151, 189, 191
Drainage and sewage disposal, 57, 61, 62-3, 66, 104, 157, 162

Economics of location, 14, 25, 49, 78-81, 111, 129, 141, 175 (See also Employment, Industries)
Economic planning, 10; economists, 185, 187
Edward I, King, 70
Electricity, 37, 38, 61, 63, 104, 109, 189
Emerson, R.W., 108, 125, 129, 130
Employment policy, 42, 79, 136, 138 (See also Economics)
Engels, F., 176
Engineering, 29, 51, 62-5, 66
Environment, human, 8, 9, 13, 14, 80, 185
Estate management, 54, 69-70, 77, 96-103, 165-6, 193

Factories: buildings, 7, 65, 109, 155, 163; sectional, 76, 81-2; size, 76, 79, 81; workshops, 97; zones for, 48, 61-4, 72-3, 76-83, 99, 103, 155, 184 (See also Industries, Trading estates)
Farm land, loss of, 41, 189, 193
Fences and hedges, 62, 75, 77, 102
Finance, of new towns, 2, 5, 31, 58-60, 86, 106-12, 148-54, 191 (See also Land, increment of value)
First Garden City Ltd., 55, 58, and passim
Flats, 5, 42-3, 45, 47, 87, 89, 111, 136; and family life, 43, 44, 47, 134, 137
Florence, Prof. Sargant, 81
Footpaths, 41, 61, 64, 66
Formby, George, 47
Fourier, F.M.C., 34, 176

Galbraith, J.K., 185
Garden city; meaning, 28, 32-3, 46, 133, 181-2; misuse of term, 39-40, 45, 182
Garden Cities of Tomorrow, 23, 25, and passim
Garden City Association (See Town and Country Planning Association)
Garden suburb, Garden village, 39-40, 181-2
Gardens, domestic, 9, 28, 33, 48, 92, 174, 175; open forecourts, 29, 75, 102; upkeep, 75, 102, 119, 120, 122, 147
Gas, 61, 63, 104, 109, 189
Geological survey, 61, 62
George, Henry, 31
Georgian Group, 29
Germany, towns in, 15, 40, 125
Gibbon, Edward, 37
Glasgow, 15, 17
Grass verges, 66
Greek cities, 37, 141, 169, 172
Green belts, 27-8, 33, 34, 48, 49, 50, 57, 68-9, 95, 133, 145, 161, 182, 188, 190, 192; history, 167-80, 194 (See also Agriculture)

Habakkuk, 192
Hamilton, Patrick, 118 n.
Hammond, J.L. and B., 14
Hampstead Garden Suburb, 39 n.

Haverfield, F.J., 194
Health, 27, 30, 49, 50, 78; services, 120, 147, 162, 183
Hertfordshire; and garden cities, 58, 87; County Council, 105
Hippodamus, 169
Horn, W.C., 68
Hospitals, 191
Housing, at garden cities, 61, 64, 65, 78, 91-4, 104; inter-war policy, 15, 42, 54, 184; future policy, 135, 138, 162-3; layout, 9, 41, 44, 47, 100-1; management, 101-2; standards, 20, 28-30, 117, 134-6; subsidies, 5, 109-112, 153-4 (See also Density, Flats, Gardens, Owner-occupiers)
Howard, Sir Ebenezer, 23-35, 56-7, 187, and passim
Howard, Keble, 37
Hugo, Victor, 13

Income Tax, 188
Industrial Revolution, 8, 10, 14, 15, 176
Industries, at Letchworth and Welwyn, 76-83, 114, 155, 184; location of, 4, 14, 42, 46, 76-83, 111, 131, 139, 155, 175 (See also Dispersal, Factories)

Jefferson, Thomas, 187
Journalists and planning, 36, 39, 44, 45
Journey to work, 7, 13, 38, 42, 48, 80, 111, 115, 117, 122, 145, 146, 185
Joyce, James, 69

Kleinstädterei, 125
Know-how, 6, 51, 70, 165-6, 189, 197

Labour, supply of, 79, 156-7, 158
Land, acquisition, 2, 60, 132, 148-9, 193; ground rents, 61, 72, 83-4, 88, 109; increment of value, 4, 31, 33, 63, 86, 106-10, 111, 158, 163-4, 183, 187, 191; unified ownership, 31, 33, 36, 48, 50, 56, 72, 106, 145, 159, 184
Land reform, 31-2, 171
Landscape gardening, 29, 30, 34, 41, 51, 62, 65-7, 75, 77, 101, 103, 129, 165, 189
Land, loss of agricultural, 189

Leasehold control, 4, 29, 31, 34, 48, 61 63, 72-6, 83-8, 96-103, 105, 187, 190 (See also Land, unified ownership)
Le Corbusier, 44, 189
Leeds, 51
Letchworth, 23, 36, 53, chaps. iii-vi, 183, 188-90, 191, and passim
Lethaby, W.R., 190
Leverhulme, Viscount, 34
Liberalism, 31
Libraries and museums, 30, 89, 127, 191
Licensed premises, 31, 73-4, 90, 94, 95, 190, 191
Light, Colonel William, 177, 178
Literature of new towns, 1, 24, 187, 195
Liverpool, 51; Speke estate, 132
Lloyd George, D., 54
Local authorities, 34, 54, 68, 74, 94, 104-6, 164, 193; as new town builders, 148-53
Local Government, Royal Commission on, 193
Local option, 30, 74, 190
Locomotive Act 1896, 37, 38
London, criticisms of, 19, 80, 123, 125; dispersal from, 51, 53, 80-1, 139, 183, 190; growth of, 15, 42, 175, 185; plans for, 24, 28, 48-51, 137, 143, 146, 152

Macaulay, T.B., 29, 125
Macquarie, Governor, 178
Manchester, 51, 132; Wythenshawe estate, 132
Marley Report, 46
Marshall, Alfred, 33
Marx, Karl, 176
Maugham, W. Somerset, 14
Meeting rooms and halls, 30, 89-90, 94, 95, 157. (See also Clubs, Community)
Molière, 187
Mountgomery, J., 194
More, Sir Thomas, 33, 34, 35, 37, 167, 172-4, 180
Moscow, 17, 115
Moses, Robert, 43
Mumford, Lewis, 3, 39 n., 49
Music, 30, 119, 121, 122, 128

INDEX

National Guilds, 68

National Trust, 41

Nationalized services, 189

Neighbourhoods, 30, 33, 34, 42, 63, 94-5, 160, 174, 188, 190

Neville, Mr. Justice, 56

New cities, 192

New South Wales, 178

New Town Agricultural Guild, 69

New Towns After the War, ix, 3, 50

New Town (Reith) Committee, 1, 2, 6, 21, 186, 193

New York, 15, 17, 181

New Zealand, cities in, 176-80

Noise, control of, 77, 102, 103

Nova Solyma, 44, 174

Nursery gardens, 62, 68

Office buildings, 4, 28, 76, 89, 99, 109; businesses, 83, 115, 190

Open spaces, 48, 185

Outbuildings, 75, 77, 102

Owen, Robert, 33, 34, 35, 174, 175-6

Owner-occupiers, 92-4

Oxford, 26

Oglethorpe, J.E., 194

Painting and sculpture, 119, 120, 122, 127

Paris, 15, 118

Parker, R. Barry, 38, 69

Parks and open spaces, 28, 41, 48, 50, 62, 90, 95, 112; park-belts, 28, 49, 50, 177-8, 182 (See also Playing Fields, Sports)

Perimeter barriers, 49, 63

Perry, Clarence, 188

Phillip, Governor, 170

Planning, evolution of, 36-52, 131-3; legislation, 17-18, 45, 98, 105, 152, 155; policy, 112, 131-40, 151, and *passim;* regional schemes, 10, 48-9, 143, 145, 163; team-work, 21, 48, 62, 69-71, 160, 165

Planning Basis, 46

Plato, 7, 33, 35, 130, 169, 172, 180

Playing Fields, 41, 90, 145, 147 (See also Parks)

Pliny the Younger, 37

Plymouth, 51

Poëte, Marcel, 194

Pomerium, 170, 172

Pope, Alexander, 96

Population: growth of, 2, 3, 133-5, 192

Port Sunlight, 38, 71

Private and public enterprise, 4, 17, 33, 36, 60, 72, 105-6, 110, 149, 152, 159, 165, 186, 187

Productivity, 185, 190

Professions, in dwelling-houses, 96-7; in new towns, 157-8

Provincialism, 19-20, 125-6

Public buildings and services, 7, 62, 72, 89-90, 112, 127-8, 132

Public houses, see Licensed premises

Public participation, 186

Purdom, C.B., ix, 55, 190

Radio and television, 20, 82, 123, 125

Railways, 56-7, 61, 63, 102-3, 122, 142, 144, 191

Reconditioning, 138-9

Redevelopment of cities, 16-17, 42, 51, 111, 138-9, 153-4, 162, 166

Regional government, 193; planning, 10, 53, 193

Reiss, R.L., 55, 70

Reith, Lord, 2, 6, 186, 193

Reps, John, 194

Research and planning, 26, 60, 113, 129-30, 143

Restaurants and hotels, 87, 89 (See also Licensed premises)

Retail trading, see Shops

Ribbon development, 41

Ricardo, Halsey, 190

Roads: lay-out, 61, 64, 65-7; lighting and maintenance, 75, 104; provision of, 64, 157, 164 (See also Transport)

Romain, Jules, 118 n.

Roman cities, 37, 170, 171, 172

Rowntree, B. Seebohm, 135

Rural areas, decline of, 27, 144, 146, 164, 175, 183, 184 (See also Agriculture)

Ruskin, John, 27, 28 n.

Saarinen, Eliel, 49

Santayana, George, 28 n.

Satellite town, meaning, 40, 46, 182, 183

INDEX

Schools: buildings, 30, 89-90, 94-95, 105, 117, 158, 164, 190
Schreiner, Olive, 172
Science, 29, 114, 120, 121, 129
Scotland, Secretary of State for, 21
Scott, Gilbert, 38
Scott Report, 45, 142, 189
Self-containment, 145
Sefton, M.R., 190
Sewerage, 65
Sharp, Granville, 194
Shaw, Norman, 34
Shops; policy, 30, 72, 83-9, 109, 115, 117; provision of buildings, 65, 109, 157, 158, 163; zoning, 62, 83, 94, 95, 96
Silchester, 37
Silkin, Lord, 188
Sites for towns, 36, 56-8, 141-8
Size of towns, 2, 15, 27, 79-81, 124, 144-5, 169, 172-5, 184, 192
Smoke and smell, 47, 77, 103
Social Cities, see Cluster Cities
Socialism and planning, 4, 14, 17, 31, 34, 176 (See also Private and public enterprise)
Sociology, 8, 25, 38, 43, 49, 113, 187
Spence, Thomas, 33
Spencer, Herbert, 33
Sports, 7, 78, 90, 94, 117 n., 119-21, 145, 185, 191 (See also Parks)
Stewart, Sir Malcolm, 46
Stockholm, 134
Stow, John, 38, 174
Suburban exodus, 8, 19, 26, 37-8, 39, 41, 45, 111, 136, 161; reactions from, 24, 41, 45, 147, 171, 184
Survey, physical, 29, 57, 61, 62, 68, 129, 160
Susanna and the Elders, 37
Swimming pools, 89
Sydney, N.S.W., 178

Taylor, Graham R., 40 n.
Taylor, W.G., ix
Terminology, 39-40, 81, 132, 181-2
Theatres, 89, 119, 121, 123, 127, 128
Tolstoy, Leo, 23, 51
Towns; growth, 15, 16, 25-7, 111, 160; limitation, 14, 28, 32, 49, 62, 69, 184 (See also Size of towns)

Town and Country Planning Association, 39, 46, 51, 56, 181
Town and Country Planning, Ministry of, 1, 21, 131, 143
Town building, pleasure of participation in, 18, 20-1, 51, 116, 157, 165, 186; personnel for, 48, 53-4, 166, 177
Town-Country Magnet, 27, 37, 176
Town Development Act, 189, 193
Trading estates, 42, 71, 76, 131
Traffic congestion, 185
Transport, 37-8, 41, 78-9, 136, 142, 155, 156, 162
Trees, choice and care of, 66-7, 189-90
Truthful James, 45

United States, 43, 74, 130, 176; city problems in, 15, 16, 32; planning in, 17, 42, 44, 172, 181, 186
Unwin, Sir Raymond, 38, 69, 70, 100
U.S.S.R., 17, 115
Uthwatt Report, 32 n., 154, 188
Utopian planning, 172-4, 176

Vienna, 43, 134
Villages, 81, 144, 181-2; institutes, 42
Voysey, C.F.A., 34

Youth centres, 191

Wakefield, E.G., 33, 172, 174, 176
War, and planning, 16, 47, 49, 82-3, 138, 139, 156
Water supply, 57, 61, 62, 65, 104, 109, 162, 189
Webb, Philip, 34
Welwyn Garden City, 3, 36, 40, 53, chaps. iii-vi, 183, 187-8, 190-91, and *passim*
Welwyn Department Store, 86-9, 190
White, M. and L., 187
Whitman, Walt, 13, 162
Whittick, Arnold, x, 187
Williams-Ellis, Clough, 41 n.
Winchelsea, 70 n.
Wright, F. Lloyd, 44, 189

Zoning, use, 28, 33, 34, 49, 62, 69, 73, 74, 76, 145; administration of, 73-4, 83, 96-8 (See also Density)

203

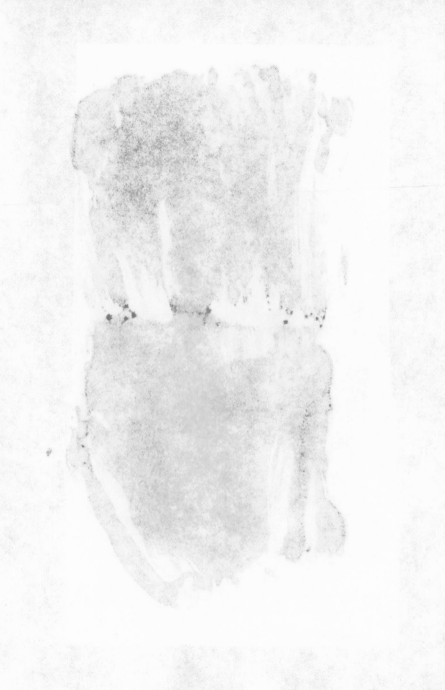

NA
9185
.076
1969

Osborn, Frederic
    James, 1885-.

Green-belt cities

DATE			

© THE BAKER & TAYLOR CO.